MW01008754

COMMITTED TO CHRIST
PROGRAM GUIDE WITH CD-ROM

Committed to Christ:
Six Steps to a Generous Life

Program Guide With CD-ROM
Lays out the basic plans for the campaign, including schedules, team roles,
sermon illustrations, worship helps, letters, and commitment cards. Art, files, schedules,
and task lists are found on the accompanying CD-ROM. 978-1-4267-4351-1

Adult Readings and Study Book
Designed for use in the six-week small group study that undergirds the program, as well
as by others participating in the program. 978-1-4267-4352-8

Small Group Leader Guide
Contains everything a leader needs to organize and run a small group or Sunday school
class in support of the program, including discussion questions, activities, and flexible
session lengths and formats. 978-1-4267-4353-5

Devotional Book: 40 Devotions for a Generous Life
Devotional companion for program participants. Each of the forty devotions
includes Scripture, a brief story or meditation, and a prayer. 978-1-4267-5488-3

DVD: Worship Videos
Designed for the worship experience, this DVD contains seven pre-worship gathering
time loops and seven lead-ins. 978-1-4267-4355-9

CD-ROM: Tweets, Posts, and Prayers
Contains devotions and prayers for use during the program to build interest and
excitement using social media: texts, Twitter, blogs, and email. 843504027681

Preview Book: Six Steps to a Generous Life
A pocket-sized book designed to introduce the congregation to the themes of the six-
week Committed to Christ experience. 978-1-4267-4690-1

Committed to Christ Kit
One of each component. 843504028886

BOB CROSSMAN

COMMITTED TO CHRIST

Six Steps to a Generous Life

Program Guide With CD-ROM

Foreword by J. Clif Christopher
With a Note by Ed Stetzer

ABINGDON PRESS
Nashville

COMMITTED TO CHRIST
PROGRAM GUIDE WITH CD-ROM
BOB CROSSMAN
COPYRIGHT © 2012 BY ABINGDON PRESS
ALL RIGHTS RESERVED.

No part of this work may be reproduced or transmitted in any form or by any means, electronic or mechanical, including photocopying and recording, or by any information storage or retrieval system, except as may be expressly permitted by the 1976 Copyright Act or in writing from the publisher. Requests for permission should be addressed in writing to Abingdon Press, 201 Eighth Avenue South, P.O. Box 801, Nashville, TN 37202-0801 or e-mailed to permissions@abingdonpress.com.

Scripture quotations marked CEB are from the Common English Bible, © Copyright 2010 by Common English Bible. All rights reserved. Used by permission. www.CommonEnglishBible.com.

Scripture quotations marked *THE MESSAGE* are taken from *THE MESSAGE*. Copyright © by Eugene H. Peterson 1993, 1994, 1995, 1996, 2000, 2001, 2002. Used by permission of NavPress Publishing Group.

Scripture quotations marked NIV are from the Holy Bible, New International Version®. Copyright © 1973, 1978, 1984, 2011 by Biblica, Inc.™ All rights reserved worldwide. www.zondervan.com. The "NIV" and "New International Version" are trademarks registered in the United States Patent and Tradmark Office by Biblica, Inc.™

Scripture quotations marked NLT are taken from the *Holy Bible,* New Living Translation, copyright © 1996, 2004, 2007. Used by permission of Tyndale House Publishers, Inc., Carol Stream, Illinois 60188. All rights reserved.

Scripture quotations marked NRSV are from the New Revised Standard Version of the Bible, copyright 1989, Division of Christian Education of the National Council of the Churches of Christ in the United States of America. Used by permission. All rights reserved.

Scripture quotations marked TNIV® are taken from the Holy Bible, Today's New International Version®. Copyright © 2001, 2005 Biblica, Inc.™ All rights reserved worldwide. Used by permission of Biblica, Inc.

This book is printed on acid-free, elemental chlorine-free paper.

ISBN 978-1-4267-4351-1

12 13 14 15 16 17 18 19 20 21 ——— 10 9 8 7 6 5 4 3 2 1

MANUFACTURED IN THE UNITED STATES OF AMERICA

So then let's also run the race that is laid out in front of us, since we have such a great cloud of witnesses surrounding us. Let's throw off any extra baggage, get rid of the sin that trips us up, and fix our eyes on Jesus, faith's pioneer and perfecter. He endured the cross, ignoring the shame, for the sake of the joy that was laid out in front of him, and sat down at the right side of God's throne. Think about the one who endured such opposition from sinners so that you won't be discouraged and you won't give up.

Hebrews 12:1-3 (CEB)

CONTENTS

FOREWORD

J. Clif Christopher
President, Horizons Stewardship

After reading my last two books, *Not Your Parents' Offering Plate* and *Whose Offering Plate Is It?* people have asked one question over and over again: If we really want to change our culture of stewardship, where is the best place to start?

My answer has always been to move toward being a high-expectation church. Begin now to establish new member classes that lay out to prospective members what true discipleship is all about. Start classes and preach sermons for your current members that lead them to high levels of commitment rather than to membership alone. Help persons, before and after they have joined, to understand what a disciple is, not what a member is. Help them to understand that we are called to give and serve, not to be given unto or served.

Bob Crossman's program, Committed to Christ: Six Steps to a Generous Life, is designed to do exactly what I describe above. Although only six weeks long (and frankly it would be difficult to change the entire church culture in six weeks), it is a great place to start. Furthermore, the program can be adapted easily as a year-round program as well, for those brave enough to venture more deeply into it.

Committed to Christ states unequivocally that being a disciple is giving all of oneself to Christ as Lord and Savior—not 10% or 20%, but 100%. Discipleship involves many commitments, none greater than the others and all necessary for a disciplined, Christ-centered life.

A disciple is one who first has a personal relationship with Jesus Christ.

A disciple is one who regularly seeks out God in prayer and devotion.

A disciple is one who reads and meditates upon the Bible.

A disciple is one who is faithful in attendance at opportunities for worship and praise.

A disciple is one who routinely shares with others what the Lord has done in their life.

A disciple is one who cheerfully returns at least a tithe of what God has given.

A disciple is one who serves the poor, the hungry, the hurting, and the lost as if that person were Christ himself.

I have worked with Bob Crossman for over twenty years. He was an extremely effective pastor and led his churches in exemplary financial stewardship and high expectations. He has been a part of Horizons Stewardship since 1998, serving as a coach and ministry strategist for hundreds of churches. It has been a pleasure for me to work with Bob in developing Committed to Christ. I hope it will be a blessing to you and your congregation.

INTRODUCTION

A dozen years ago I was the pastor of a new church. The church was only five years old. We had grown to 450 in worship, and I had witnessed 200 professions of faith, 100 reaffirmations of faith, more than 200 baptisms, and a church family of over 1,000 people. We also witnessed transfers of membership from over 250 congregations representing 23 different denominations.

Though it was a good start, all of us felt it was time for the church to step up to the next level. However, I had two concerns.

First, I believed it was time for the church to begin adding program and support staff, but the financial resources were simply not there. In fact, that year we added our first paid staff in music and children's ministry, which increased the church's operating budget by $50,000; in spite of that, the offering showed only a modest increase that spring, and we were headed toward a $50,000 deficit for the year. A slow-motion financial train wreck was happening in front of my eyes.

Second, while the congregation was filled with excitement over the church's growth and the weekly addition of new households into the church family, most members of the congregation did not have a clear, articulate, or compelling sense of exactly what the Lord expected of them as disciples.

About a fifth of the adults in the church had participated in the nine-month program *Disciple: Becoming Disciples Through Bible Study,* written by my colleague Richard Wilke. A smaller number of the *Disciple* graduates had also completed the second and third year of that amazing program. However, if you had asked most of those graduates what the Lord expects of those who seek to be faithful disciples, they might have summarized what they had learned in *Disciple,* but they might not have been able to answer effectively.

As pastor of this fast-growing congregation, I was concerned that a significant number of them were not fully engaged in a journey toward becoming deeply devoted disciples of Jesus Christ.

"Tell me about your stewardship program."

Around that time, I traveled to Oklahoma City to visit my friend Dr. Norman Neaves, founding pastor of Church of the Servant. Over a cup of coffee I shared the story of my church and the financial concerns at that time, with a $1,000 shortfall each Sunday.

His reply was simple: "Tell me about your stewardship program."

I answered, "Oh, we do about the same or more than most churches. We emphasize financial stewardship during the first two weeks of November. A letter is mailed to the membership with an enclosed pledge card. The following Sunday, the church treasurer speaks for a few minutes from the pulpit, asking everyone to take the card home and to pray about their decision. He then invites the congregation to bring the card back the next week. My sermon that Sunday is on the subject of giving."

After a long pause, Norman asked, "Is that all?" My silence and puzzled look in response revealed volumes.

Norman began to share with me his understanding of stewardship. He said that our task as pastors is to invite the congregation, and the mission field that surrounds it, not only to accept Jesus Christ as Lord and Savior but to grow each year toward becoming deeply devoted disciples of Jesus Christ. He went on to say that he was looking for a way to begin inviting his congregation annually to join in that journey, one step at a time. He believed that the journey consisted of commitments involving prayers, presence in worship, financial gifts, and service. He also believed that the Lord calls each of us to journey closer and closer to the cross, and to reach back and invite others to join us in that journey.

Committed to Christ: Six Steps to a Generous Life was born that day. I developed the program over the next six months, designing a strategy to invite churches to begin the journey, step by step, across a broad spectrum of discipleship.

My church implemented the basic plan of Committed to Christ and within a year the number of pledging households increased by 17%, the amount pledged increased 58%, and the actual offering receipts grew by 64%.

More importantly, the congregation adopted the spirit and approach of Committed to Christ and accepted the challenge of climbing at least one step each year. The vitality of the church surged forward as commitments were made and kept: first and foremost to Jesus Christ, then to daily prayer, Bible reading, worship, witness, financial giving, and service. The congregation became so engaged in the journey that they insisted that Committed to Christ be repeated year after year, as they continued to grow and step up toward becoming deeply devoted disciples.

"The only time the Church thinks of me is when they want money."

There are many stewardship programs designed for a fall stewardship event in a local church, focusing almost exclusively on financial gifts to the church. One problem with this approach is that in most churches, the only time every household is contacted in person or by direct mail is to ask for financial gifts. Members are often correct when they say, "The only time the church thinks of me is when they want money." That should never be the case.

The call to Christian discipleship is far broader than the typical fall stewardship campaign. I believe that Committed to Christ: Six Steps to a Generous Life is closer to the full range of invitations the Lord makes to each one of us who seeks to be a disciple.

One of the responsibilities of leadership in the church is to invite the congregation and the mission field that surrounds the church not only to accept Jesus Christ as Lord and Savior but to grow each year toward becoming deeply devoted disciples of Jesus. Committed to Christ is one way to begin inviting the congregation, step by step, to join in that journey.

In the program, we use tried-and-true methods that are found in many different financial stewardship programs. The unique element that we add is the level and number of commitments, beginning first and foremost with an invitation to commit to Christ. We then move on to six steps of commitment that follow naturally, with equal emphasis placed on each of these six different areas of Christian discipleship.

During worship, members of the congregation will be invited to make a commitment to take one or more steps in the following areas:

On the introductory Sunday:
- Becoming a committed follower and disciple of Jesus Christ

On the six Sundays that follow:
- Daily prayer
- Bible reading
- Faithful worship attendance
- Witness by sharing the good news of Jesus Christ

- Financial gifts growing to the 10% tithe
- Hands-on service in Jesus' name

At the end of this six-week stewardship and discipleship emphasis, members can no longer say, "The only time the church thinks of me is when they want money." Instead, they can truthfully say, "My church expects a lot."

CHEESY GIVING?

Ed Stetzer

Throughout life we are presented with opportunities to exercise good stewardship related to finances. Sometimes we make good decisions and sometimes we make bad decisions, but we seek always to honor Christ in the decisions we make. An interaction with one of my children about snack food provided humorous but real insight into this struggle.

Recently, around the time I was teaching on stewardship at our church, I was drawn into an argument with my middle daughter over an empty box of Cheez-Its in our cabinet. Convinced that I eaten all those tasty little crackers, my daughter became obsessed with getting her own Cheez-Its to replace them. Her actions were like those of a person convinced there were no more Cheez-Its in the world! The truth was, she did not believe that her father could or would give her more of this favorite food.

During the teaching series at our church, we created a big box of Cheez-Its to put on stage to serve as a metaphor. We realized that, for some of us, fear (of not having something) leads to greed (I want that thing) leads to idolatry (I worship that thing) leads to bondage (it rules and imprisons me). My daughter's reaction to the empty box is an example of our own lack of faith that our Father can provide for our needs. It also illustrates how anything can derail our willingness to honor God by being good financial stewards.

Ed Stetzer is President of LifeWay Research, one of the best and most-quoted Christian research organizations in the world. He has planted churches in multiple states; trained pastors across the U.S. and on six continents; and taught at 14 seminaries. Author or co-author of 12 books, Stetzer is a leading voice among evangelicals. He is a contributing editor or columnist for several publications, including Christianity Today, Outreach Magazine, The Christian Post, *and* Facts and Trends.

I.
Understanding
the Program

1.
PROGRAM APPROACH AND STRUCTURE

Committed to Christ: Six Steps to a Generous Life is not simply an annual financial campaign for the local church. Rather, it is a holistic discipleship emphasis that places financial giving within the context of what the Lord expects of those who seek to be faithful disciples. The focus is not on the church's needs, but rather upon each individual's need to respond generously to the saving grace of Jesus Christ.

Committed to Christ is an invitation to every household in the congregation to begin and continue a lifelong journey that will raise their level of commitment to Christ by focusing on each of six areas of discipleship.

In his book *Renovate or Die,* Bob Farr paraphrases the level of expectation in the traditional church as "Come a little bit, do a little bit, give a little bit, and say a whole lot."[1] Churches that are seeking to leave that old paradigm behind and become high-expectation churches may find that Committed to Christ is a natural introduction to the high expectations that the Lord has of all who seek to be disciples.

In 2011, George Barna released an assessment of how America's faith has shifted between 1991 and 2011. The study showed that several religious behaviors experienced statistically significant changes among adults. Bible reading during the course of a typical week has declined from 45% to 40%; serving through volunteering, donating any time during a typical week, has declined from 27% to 19%; small group attendance has declined from 23% to 15% on a typical Sunday; and worship attendance has dropped from 49% to 40%.[2] Committed to Christ works to reverse these declining trends within your church.

The program is introduced then carried out over a six-week period. During the introductory sermon and worship, the people of your congregation will be invited to join together on a journey that begins, first and foremost, with a deeper commitment to Christ.

Then, in response to the saving grace of Jesus Christ, each household is invited to join a journey toward faithful discipleship in six core areas that are given equal emphasis, focusing on one per week:

1. Prayer
2. Bible reading
3. Worship
4. Witness
5. Financial giving
6. Service

During this six-week period, the congregation will build and strengthen their commitment to Christ through worship, small groups, and other activities. With each step, people will be asked to think seriously about and set goals for that particular aspect of discipleship. The six steps begin with interior activities and move outward.

> *"Very truly I tell you, whoever hears my word and believes him who sent me has eternal life and will not be judged but has crossed over from death to life."*
>
> John 5:24 (TNIV)

For each of the six steps, as well as for the initial and all-important step of committing to Christ, you'll be asking the people in your congregation to fill out a commitment card. Each card poses a question at the top, then offers a range of responses, from no commitment to strong and continuing commitment. The cards will be passed out and discussed each Sunday, then filled out and returned that same Sunday. You'll find copies of these cards in Appendix C of this program guide, as well as electronic files for producing them on the CD-ROM at the back of this book, which can be printed out at church or taken to a local printer. Cards are included for commitments from youth and children as well.

In addition to commitment cards, this program guide and the companion CD-ROM provides everything needed for the introductory worship and the following six weeks: sermon ideas, worship suggestions and videos, survey forms, sample letters or e-mails, and more. In addition, everything you need for small group activities are in the *Adult Readings and Study Book* and the *Small Group Leader Guide*.

The "generous life" in Committed to Christ refers to its invitation to live and serve generously in response to the saving grace of the Lord, not as an obligation but as a joyous act of devotion. This balanced and generous life, arising out of a commitment to Jesus Christ, flows through every facet of daily living, beginning with prayer.

Committed to Christ, through years of workshops and consultations, has been used in congregations across the country, producing great fruit in church after church. Here are some of the reasons why:

- The program is holistic, with each of the six steps anchored in the context of an initial commitment to Jesus Christ as Lord and Savior.
- The six invitational steps are perceived by the congregation to reflect what the Lord expects of those who seek to be faithful followers. These commitments have historically framed the church's primary expectations and are worthy of giving one's life to.
- The program places equal emphasis on each of the six steps, clearly communicating that this is not simply "about money."
- The steps are realistic and achievable for each participant. Persons who are new to the faith will find introductory, first-step invitations that are engaging and challenging. The saints, who have attended worship and Sunday school for their entire lives, will find advanced steps that invite them to grow not just incrementally but in the quality of their relationship with God and in response to the Lord's expectations of those who seek to be deeply devoted disciples.
- By the very structure and layout of the program, the congregation understands that they are being invited on a journey with their fellow believers, step by step. Committed to Christ is not a simple six-week emphasis that is "over when it's over." Rather, the program presents a journey worthy of a lifetime. It is an invitation to begin intentionally, step by step, month by month, year by year, a journey toward holiness, toward sanctification, toward winning the only race worth winning.

I have fought the good fight, finished the race, and kept the faith. At last the champion's wreath that is awarded for righteousness is waiting for me. The Lord, who is the righteous judge, is going to give it to me on that day. He's giving it not only to me but also to all those who have set their heart on waiting for his appearance.
2 Timothy 4:7-8 (NLT)

- There is a ripple effect. When church members make a commitment in any of the six areas and then seek to be faithful to that commitment, they tend to grow and mature in the other steps as well.

Committed to Christ has been tested, revised, and retested. If you follow the program faithfully your church will achieve positive results. In the few cases where results were disappointing, the churches with less-desirable results cut corners or altered the program. Please resist the temptation to make changes or omit any portion of this program, as it may drastically reduce the program's effectiveness.

2.
COMMITMENT TO CHRIST

During the introductory sermon and worship of Committed to Christ: Six Steps to a Generous Life, the people of your congregation will be invited to join together on a journey that begins with a deeper commitment to Christ.

For all have sinned and fall short of the glory of God, and all are justified freely by his grace through the redemption that came by Christ Jesus.
Romans 3:23-24 (TNIV)

This introductory Sunday reflects the primary mission of the church: to invite people to be disciples and have a positive, growing, and vital relationship with Jesus Christ as Savior and Lord. This kind of discipleship is not like a diploma that is earned, framed, and hung on the wall for all to admire. Christian discipleship is different from that. Becoming a Christian disciple is more like a marriage than a marriage certificate.

Many disciples report that their early faith journey was made up of several different phases, or seasons. There was an initial season of being introduced to Jesus Christ, when they encountered Christ through the witness or experience of trusted family or friends. Intrigued by this initial encounter, they entered a season of discovering the teachings and life of Christ. Often they report a season of conversations that took place with trusted family or friends about the nature and depth of a saving relationship with Christ, and the implications that this might have on their own lifestyle, relationships, and future. This season of discovery most often included attendance at Christian worship services and initial attempts to read the story of Jesus in the Bible. Then some hours, months, or years later they entered a season of decision to accept a relationship with Jesus Christ. After this first big decision, in the course of their lives there were daily decisions to continue the relationship with Christ, and occasional intense moments of rededication and renewal of that saving relationship.

God demonstrates his own love for us in this: While we were still sinners, Christ died for us.

Romans 5:8 (TNIV)

In some Christian traditions, the initial faith journey described above is clearly articulated with precise steps and a set of expectations along with each step. In some congregations, for example, it is truthfully said that "everyone in Miss Hester's fifth grade Sunday school class makes a personal commitment to accept Christ before the year is over." In other Christian traditions, this initial faith journey is understood to be more of a mystery, with the journey entirely dependent upon God's intervention. In still other Christian traditions, this initial faith journey is expected to take place within the home as parents teach their children by word and example.

Recognizing the differences among these unique traditions, the introductory Sunday worship and sermon in the Committed to Christ program offer an invitation for every household to begin, renew, or re-engage in a positive, growing, and vital relationship with Jesus Christ as Savior and Lord.

Because if you confess with your mouth "Jesus is Lord" and in your heart you have faith that God raised him from the dead, you will be saved. Trusting with the heart leads to righteousness, and confessing with the mouth leads to salvation. The scripture says, All who have faith in him won't be put to shame. There is no distinction between Jew and Greek, because the same Lord is Lord of all, who gives richly to all who call on him. All who call on the Lord's name will be saved.

Romans 10:9-13 (CEB)

The invitation to commit to Christ is not a static or one-time event; it is the beginning of a life-long journey. Faithful disciples are continually asking, "What does the Lord expect of me?"

With this in mind, what is involved in the journey from new disciple to deeply devoted disciple of Jesus Christ?

John Wesley, Anglican priest and founder of the eighteenth-century Methodist movement, is known for his teaching on this subject. He taught that faithful Christians live with a desire to follow the pattern or lifestyle of Jesus perfectly and to live in harmony with Jesus' teachings. Wesley believed that we are to strive constantly for this goal, yet few if any fully achieve it in this life.

The Apostle Paul compared this striving to the work of an athlete training for an event. In the same way, Christians are to be actively engaged in a never-ending process that begins with our first awareness of Jesus Christ and continues for the rest of this earthly life.

All good athletes train hard. They do it for a gold medal that tarnishes and fades. You're after one that's gold eternally. I don't know about you, but I'm running hard for the finish line. I'm giving it everything I've got. No sloppy living for me! I'm staying alert and in top condition. I'm not going to get caught napping, telling everyone else all about it and then missing out myself.

1 Corinthians 9:24-27 (*THE MESSAGE*)

The program's introductory Sunday, focusing on your congregation's commitment to Christ, takes place prior to the six weeks of the program. Because of its importance, you may want to schedule this introductory Sunday a few weeks before the program, to help your congregation prepare for the commitments they will be considering during the program itself.

However you choose to handle the scheduling, on that introductory Sunday the commitment card will ask the question, "Will you choose to be a committed follower and disciple of Jesus Christ?" The card offers seven possible responses to the question, starting with no commitment and then moving to an initial fleeting hope that will challenge the new believer, and finally building to responses that will challenge the mature disciple:

- No, today I am not ready to make a commitment.
- No, but maybe someday.
- No, but I want to with all my heart.
- Yes, today, for the first time, I accept Jesus Christ as my Savior.
- Yes, I have already accepted Jesus Christ. The year was about _____.
- Yes, and someday I will be ready for an even closer walk with the Lord.
- Yes, and today I am ready for a closer walk with the Lord, growing to include the following:

Jesus is my guiding light, my compass, my lighthouse. I will ask the Lord for that "peace that passes all understanding." I will strive for my speech and behavior to please the Lord. I will strive for my attitudes, values, and thoughts to please the Lord. I will be passionate about the Lord as the priority of my life. I will strive to be able to explain clearly what I believe and why. I look forward to having a constant awareness of the Lord's presence. I will strive for others to see Christ in my life, words, and actions. At each major decision of my life, I will ask, "What would Jesus have me do?" I will bring the Lord into my marriage, my family, and all my relationships. I will allow Christ to love others through me, even those who are different from me.

This introductory Sunday, including the filling out of the commitment card, lays a solid foundation for the six Sundays of Committed to Christ.

Many of the Samaritans from that town believed in him because of the woman's testimony, "He told me everything I ever did." So when the Samaritans came to him, they urged him to stay with them, and he stayed two days. And because of his words many more became believers. They said to the woman, "We no longer believe just because of what you said; now we have heard for ourselves, and we know that this man really is the Savior of the world."

John 4:39-42 (TNIV)

3.
THE SIX STEPS

Committed to Christ invites each household, in response to the saving grace of Jesus Christ, to join a journey toward faithful discipleship in six core areas: daily prayer, Bible reading, faithful worship attendance, witnessing to others about the saving Good News of Jesus Christ, financial giving growing to the biblical standard of the 10% tithe, and giving of time through hands-on service.

1. Prayer

During the first formal week of the program, each household is invited to climb the first step in their journey toward greater commitment to Christ. This step is about prayer—how it can transform life and what it is all about. We suggest prayer as the first step because if the people of your congregation are going to have a personal relationship with the Lord, it is going to begin with prayer.

This is not a step toward earning one's salvation, but rather a step toward a generous life in response to salvation already received from Christ.

In worship, small group study, and devotions, the people of your congregation will be invited to think seriously about and set goals for the growth of their prayer lives. They will learn that one of the amazing truths of Christianity is that God desires to be in relationship with each of us through prayer. The holy habit of daily prayer not only reminds us of our relationship with the Lord but also becomes an open channel to receive encouragement and direction as we begin this spiritual journey to live and serve in Jesus' name.

A good way to begin the program and help the people of your congregation focus on their prayer life is to lift up the devotional book that comes with this program, Committed to Christ: 40 Devotions for a Generous Life. This devotional book is keyed to the themes and schedule of the overall program, beginning with commitment to Christ and moving through the six steps of commitment.

In addition to the devotional book, the program includes devotions and prayers for use with social media, provided on the CD-ROM that comes with the program kit. This CD-ROM is titled *Tweets, Posts, and Prayers,* and it will be useful both for the individuals in your congregation and for the church staff and program leadership. These short devotional pieces can be posted on Twitter, Facebook, or your church Web site.

Hear my voice when I call, LORD;
be merciful to me and answer me.
My heart says of you, "Seek his face!"
Your face, LORD, I will seek.

Psalm 27:7-8 (TNIV)

John Wesley, in a sermon entitled "The Scripture Way of Salvation," spoke about the "work" of growing and maturing as a disciple of Jesus Christ. He spoke of this "work" as having two parts: "works of piety" and "works of mercy."[3]

Works of piety include those activities that touch our own hearts and build our faith and trust in God, such as worship; receiving the Lord's Supper; public prayer, family prayer, and praying in secret; and searching the Bible by hearing, reading, and meditating on the Scriptures.

Works of mercy include those things that touch the hearts of others and build their faith, such as: giving food and clothing to the needy; welcoming the stranger; visiting in prisons and hospitals; teaching the Bible; encouraging sinners to turn away from sin; strengthening the faith of those who are filled with doubt; and contributing in any manner to save souls from death.

As suggested by Wesley, the first step of commitment to a growing prayer life is not only a lifelong journey but also offered in context with a variety of other commitments that faithful disciples make as they strive to grow and mature as disciples of Jesus Christ.

The prayer commitment card asks the question, "Are you ready to grow in your prayer life?" It includes responses geared to the new believer as well as to the mature disciple. The responses focus in part on the frequency of prayer, and in part on the quality of prayer life.

Some of your people will only be ready to make one commitment, while others will be ready to make several commitments to grow in prayer. Respondents may check as many of the following as they would like.

- Today, I am not ready to make a commitment to pray.
- Beginning today, I will pray when I am in a worship service.
- Beginning today, I will pray every time I am facing a difficult decision.
- Beginning today, I will try to pray daily.
- Beginning today, I will pray daily, using a devotional guide.
- Beginning today, I will pray daily, remembering the prayer requests shared in worship.
- Beginning today, I will pray daily, using the weekly prayer list from the church.
- Beginning today, I will pray daily, setting aside fifteen minutes for daily devotional time.
- Beginning today, I will pray daily and be in the church prayer chain or prayer group.
- Prayer will be a priority in my life, growing to include the following:

I will surround my family and friends with prayer. I will surround my church with prayer. Through prayer, I will find strength, power, and direction to face the week. Through prayer, I will trust God with my life, my family, my job, my finances, and my immediate and eternal future. Through prayer, I will learn to love God with all my heart and to love my neighbors.

New believers and pre-Christians may struggle with the program's invitation to pray for the first time. Their initial commitment may be modest, but it could prove to be the first step toward a lifelong journey toward a deeply devoted prayer life.

Those who have prayed before may be ready to accept an invitation to pray in worship or when facing difficult decisions. This modest commitment may be the first step toward bringing all the major decisions of life to the foot of the Cross and seeking guidance from the Lord.

These first two steps of prayer may seem simple and childlike, but childlike steps are necessary before learning to walk. These childlike steps in prayer introduce a journey toward trusting God with our life, our family, our spouse, our job, our finances, our immediate and eternal future. These first steps may be followed by second, third—an entire lifetime of steps toward an increasingly deep and mature prayer life.

Others will find challenge in the third level of commitment: trying to pray daily. Through worship, small group study, and suggested Twitter and blog prayers, your people will be invited to consider making this holy habit of prayer at a set time each day—perhaps when first waking up, driving to work, in the afternoon commute home, as their last words every evening, or by the addition of grace at every meal.

Many in your congregation will already have the holy habit of daily prayer and will now be ready for a more structured devotional time, using the devotional book and CD-ROM provided with this program.

Some in your congregation will appreciate the invitation to include the prayer requests shared in worship or to use the weekly prayer list from the church. As a result, you may find them listening more closely during worship to shared prayer concerns, or reading more carefully the weekly prayer list provided by your church office.

The next two responses invite a more structured commitment to prayer—setting aside prayer time, praying daily, and participating in the church prayer chain or prayer group.

The last and most ambitious commitment is focused primarily on the quality of a mature prayer life, including surrounding one's family and church with prayer and personally using prayer to find strength, power, and direction to face the week.

On this Sunday devoted to prayer, you and the Follow-through Task Group (see Part 2 of this program guide) will want to set up a display in the foyer to provide information about prayer groups and devotional activities in your church, to help people keep this week's commitments faithfully. On Ministry Celebration Sunday, the final week of the program, these activities and groups can be presented again, along with handouts and samples of follow-up resources for people to use in the weeks and months after the program concludes. (See the CD-ROM at the back of this book, under 6. Tools and Helps: Follow-up Resources.)

2. Bible Reading

During the second formal week of the program, each household is invited to climb another step in their journey toward greater commitment to Christ. This step is about the holy habit of hearing, reading, and reflecting on the words of Scripture found in the Bible and how it can transform our lives by fostering a growing personal relationship with the Lord.

As with prayer, this is not a step toward earning one's salvation, but rather a step toward living a generous life in response to salvation already received from Christ.

> Theologian and Wesley scholar Albert Outler once said, "The Bible is the story of what God has been doing and will always be doing on earth for his people. It is the story of what he has designed us for and what he rightfully expects from us. It is the story of what we can count on from God: covenant making and covenant keeping on God's part, and covenant making and covenant breaking on our side. It is a book that helps us become truly human."[4]

This second step is more than a simple invitation to read the Bible; it is also an invitation to put the words of the Bible into practice. It can lead to a lifelong journey, in context with a variety of other commitments faithful disciples make as they strive to grow and mature as a disciple of Jesus Christ.

Do not merely listen to the word, and so deceive yourselves. Do what it says. Those who listen to the word but do not do what it says are like people who look at their faces in a mirror and, after looking at themselves, go away and immediately forget what they look like. But those who look intently into the perfect law that gives freedom, and continue in it—not forgetting what they have heard, but doing it—they will be blessed in what they do.

James 1:22-25 (TNIV)

The commitment card this week asks the question, "Are you ready to climb one or more steps in your Bible reading?" Some of your people will only be ready to make one commitment; others will be ready to make several commitments. Respondents may check as many of the following as they would like.

- No, I am not ready to make a commitment today.
- No, I am not ready to start, but I want to with all my heart.
- Yes, I will read the Bible sometimes.
- Yes, I will read the Bible frequently.
- Yes, I will read the Bible on a daily schedule . . . and I am ready for a structured plan of Bible reading (check all that apply).
- Yes, and I will begin today reading the entire New Testament.
- Yes, and I will begin today reading the entire Old Testament.
- Yes, and I will sign up for a weekly small group to study the Bible with others.
- Yes, and I will look for additional opportunities to join a Bible study.
- Reading the Bible will be a priority in my life, growing to include the following:

I will strive for my daily life to reflect the teachings of the Bible. I will surround my family and friends with Scripture. Through reading the Bible I will find strength, power, and direction to face the week.

Some will choose the first or second response, which allows a person to decline honestly yet leave the door open for a future commitment. Others, including new believers and pre-Christians, will struggle with the invitation to read the Bible for the first time yet still want to make a lower level of commitment to read the Bible on occasion. This response, though modest, may be the beginning of a life-long journey toward a deeply devoted understanding of the Bible.

Those who occasionally read the Bible may be ready to accept an invitation to read it more frequently. Again, this is a modest commitment, but it can be the first step toward looking for guidance in the holy Scriptures when faced with life's major decisions.

These first two levels of commitment to Bible reading may seem basic for those who have been reading the Bible for decades. However, before becoming a scholar of the Word, one must first simply commit to read the Bible.

Others will decide to take up the challenge offered in the next commitment level: reading the Bible on a daily schedule, perhaps first thing each morning, during lunch break, together as a household each evening, as the last words they read every evening, or by reading a portion at every meal.

Many in your congregation will already have the holy habit of daily Bible reading and will be ready for a more structured study and reflection time. The invitation to structured Bible study will allow you to highlight ongoing Bible study opportunities within the Church, such as in small groups on Sunday morning or during the week; and major Bible study opportunities, such as the *Disciple* Bible study program, which has proven to be transformational for many churches, lifting them to a higher level of faith and practice.

This week's focus on Bible reading will also enable you to highlight daily Scripture passages that you already may be posting on Facebook, Twitter, or your church Web site, as well as various one-year or multi-year plans for reading the entire Bible. For your convenience, we are providing a form that can be useful to chart Bible reading. (See Appendix C. Samples and Forms, as well as the CD-ROM in the back of this book.)

The final response offered on this week's commitment card focuses not so much on the quantity as on the quality of mature Bible reading: promising to lead a life that reflects the Scriptures, surrounding one's family with Scripture, and finding strength, power, and direction through Bible reading to face the week.

As with the previous week, you and the Follow-through Task Group (see Part 2 of this program guide) are invited to set up a display in the foyer to provide information about Bible study groups and activities in your church, to help people keep this week's commitments faithfully. On Ministry Celebration Sunday, the final week of the program, these groups and activities can be presented again, along with handouts and samples of follow-up resources for people to use in the weeks and months following the program. (See the CD-ROM at the back of this book, under 6. Tools and Helps: Follow-up Resources.)

3. Worship

During the third formal week of the program, each household is invited to climb another step in their journey toward greater commitment to Christ. This step is about worship—what it is about and how faithful worship attendance can transform your life.

This is not a step toward earning one's salvation, but rather a step toward living a generous life in response to salvation already received from Christ.

I was glad when they said unto me,
"Let us go into the house of the Lord."
Psalm 122:1 (KJV)

At the heart of Christian life we find worship. Through worship we express our theology, define our identity, and commune with our maker. When we encounter God in worship, we are formed and transformed as his people.[5]

Just like a deer that craves
streams of water,
my whole being craves you, God.
My whole being thirsts for God,
for the living God.
When will I come and see God's face?
Psalm 42:1-2 (CEB)

The commitment card this week asks the question, "Are you ready to grow in your worship attendance?" The list of responses is directed toward the new believer as well as the mature disciple. The responses focus in part on the frequency but also on the quality of worship. Some of your people will only be ready to make one commitment, while others will be ready to make several commitments. Respondents may check as many of the following as they would like.

- Today, I am not ready to make a commitment.
- I will attend worship three to six times a year.
- I will attend worship once a month.
- I will attend worship twice a month.
- I will attend worship three times a month.
- I will attend worship four times a month.

- As my health permits, I will never miss worship.
- Worship will be a priority in my life, growing to include the following:

I will be passionate about worship as a true priority of my life. Bad weather, sports, or holidays will not keep me from attending worship. I will prepare the day before, so that I can arrive at worship without last-minute rushing. I will warmly greet those who sit around me. I will surround my friends and family with worship. Through worship I will seek to find strength, power, and direction to face the week.

In response to this Sunday's question, some of your people will only be ready to make one commitment, while others will be ready to make several commitments to grow in worship.

New believers and pre-Christians may be unwilling to commit to weekly worship, and so they may choose a worship frequency with which they feel comfortable—a few times a year, or once a month. This initial commitment is modest, but it may prove to be the first step toward a life-long journey toward a deeply devoted worship life.

Many in your congregation will already be attending worship and are now ready to take the next step, committing to attend worship three or four times a month—or even, as health permits, never to miss worship.

The final response on this week's commitment card is focused primarily on the quality of a mature worship life: being passionate about worship as a priority in life, preparing in advance for worship, greeting fellow worshipers warmly, surrounding family and friends with worship, and finding through worship the strength, power, and direction to face the week.

This Sunday, you and the Follow-through Task Group (see Part 2 of this program guide) are invited to set up a display in the foyer to provide information about worship groups and activities in your church, to help people keep this week's commitments faithfully. On Ministry Celebration Sunday, the final week of the program, these groups and activities can be presented again, along with handouts and samples of follow-up resources for people to use in the weeks and months after the program. (See the CD-ROM at the back of this book, under 6. Tools and Helps: Follow-up Resources.)

Let us keep a firm grip on the promises that keep us going. He always keeps his word. Let's see how inventive we can be in encouraging love and helping out, not avoiding worshiping together as some do, but spurring each other on, especially as we see the big Day approaching.

Hebrews 10:23-25 (*THE MESSAGE*)

4. Witness

During the fourth week of the program, each household is invited to climb one more step in their journey toward greater commitment to Christ. This step is about witnessing—what lifelong commitment to witness means, how it can transform lives, and how we can invite others to experience a commitment to Christ. The Lord calls each of us to journey closer and closer to the cross, but he also calls each of us to reach back and invite others to join us in the journey. If the people of your congregation are going to have a growing personal relationship with the Lord, it will involve witnessing and sharing the good news of Jesus Christ.

Be wise in the way you act toward outsiders; make the most of every opportunity. Let your conversation be always full of grace, seasoned with salt, so that you may know how to answer everyone.

Colossians 4:5-6 (TNIV)

This is not a step toward earning one's salvation, but rather a step toward living a generous life in response to salvation already received from Christ. It is more than a simple invitation to witness once; rather, it is a call to discover a lifestyle in which witnessing is an integral part of daily life and every relationship. This week is an invitation for new disciples to share their faith with others for the first time. For mature disciples, this week invites a commitment to make witness a priority in their lives.

"Therefore, go and make disciples of all nations, baptizing them in the name of the Father and of the Son and of the Holy Spirit, teaching them to obey everything that I've commanded you. Look, I myself will be with you every day until the end of this present age."

Matthew 28:19-20 (CEB)

The commitment card this week asks the question, "Will you witness and share your faith in Christ?" The list of responses is directed toward the new believer as well as the mature disciple. The responses focus in part on the frequency of witnessing, but also on the quality of the witness commitment. Some of your people will only be ready to make one commitment, while others will be ready to make several commitments. Respondents may check as many of the following as they would like.

- No, today I'm not ready to make a commitment.
- Not now, but maybe someday.

- Not now, but I want to with all my heart.
- Yes, I will share my faith sometimes.
- Yes, I will share my faith frequently.
- Yes, I will look for daily opportunities to share about Jesus.
- Yes, and telling others about Jesus will become a priority in my life, to include the following:

I will grow in my lifestyle so that pre-Christians will see Christ in all my words and actions. I will grow in my faith so that I will have the confidence to share it. I will watch for new neighbors and invite them to worship. I will pray for the salvation of specific non-Christian people. I will be praying for specific people to attend my small group. I will warmly greet and visit with worship guests who sit by me in worship. After someone has accepted Christ, I will continue to offer my friendship and support.

New believers and pre-Christians may struggle with the invitation to witness for the first time and can respond simply with "Not now, but maybe someday" or "Not now, but I want to with all my heart." These responses indicate an openness to witnessing opportunities in the future. These may prove to be the first steps in a lifelong journey toward witnessing in Jesus' name.

Those who occasionally or sporadically witness may be ready to share their faith "sometimes." Again, this represents a first step toward actually witnessing, perhaps for the first time. Others may be willing to go further, sharing their faith "frequently" or even "daily."

The final response listed on this week's commitment card is focused primarily on the quality of a mature life of witnessing, to include making witness a priority in life; trying to embody Christ in words and actions; growing in faith to have the confidence to share it; sharing the good news of Christ with neighbors; praying for specific people to attend small group meetings, warmly greeting guests in worship; and continuing to offer friendship and support to new Christians and new church members.

Focusing on being a witness will allow you and the Follow-through Task Group (see Part 2 of this program guide) to highlight a wide variety of opportunities in your church that may already be in place around welcoming, hospitality, greeting, or serving as an usher. This is also an opportunity to highlight service opportunities as part of a system for following up with guests and first-time visitors. The Follow-through Task Group may suggest and organize short-term classes designed to teach people how to witness effectively and how to invite others to worship.

On Ministry Celebration Sunday, the final week of the program, these groups and activities can be presented again, along with handouts and samples of follow-up resources for people to use in the weeks and months following the program. (See the CD-ROM at the back of this book, under 6. Tools and Helps: Follow-up Resources.)

> *My mouth will repeat*
> *your righteous acts*
> *and your saving deeds all day long.*
>
> Psalm 71:15a (CEB)

5. Financial Giving

During the fifth formal week of the program, each household is invited to climb another step in their journey toward greater commitment to Christ. This step is about financial giving, growing toward the biblical standard of a 10% tithe—what giving is all about and how it can transform lives. If the people of your congregation are going to have a personal relationship with the Lord, it is going to involve faithful and proportional giving of their financial resources.

> *In this way we remember the Lord Jesus' words: "It is more blessed to give than to receive."*
>
> Acts 20:35b (CEB)

As with the other commitments, this is not a step toward earning one's salvation, but rather a step toward living a generous life in response to salvation already received from Christ.

> *Your way of life should be free from the love of money, and you should be content with what you have. After all, he has said, I will never leave you or abandon you. This is why we confidently say,*
> > *The Lord is my helper,*
> > *and I won't be afraid.*
> > *What can people do to me?*
>
> Hebrews 13:5-6 (CEB)

Giving lies at the heart of the Christian life. It is in giving that we express our theology and define our identity. It's been said that the Bible includes 500 verses on prayer, fewer than

500 verses on faith, and more than 2,000 verses on money and what money buys.[6]

Jesus talked a lot about money, and I'm confident that the synagogue offering increased in every town where Jesus taught.

> *"No household servant can serve two masters. Either you will hate the one and love the other, or you will be loyal to the one and have contempt for the other. You cannot serve God and wealth." The Pharisees, who were money-lovers, heard all this and sneered at Jesus.*
>
> Luke 16:13-14 (CEB)

The commitment card this week asks the question, "Are you ready to grow one or more steps in your giving?" The list of responses is directed toward the new believer as well as the mature disciple. The responses focus in part on the amount of the gift, but also on the quality of the gift. Some of your people will only be ready to make one commitment, while others will be ready to make several commitments. Respondents may check as many of the following as they would like.

- No, I am (we are) not ready to commit at this time.
- Yes, I am (we are) ready to commit as follows:

General Fund

January 1 to December 31 of the coming year:

$ _____ every ☐ week ☐ month ☐ quarter ☐ year

for an annual total of $ _____ to the General Fund.

Optional: Check all that apply.

This is a tithe (10%) of my (our) income.

This is _____% of my (our) income.

In the years ahead, with God's help, I (we) will step up toward tithing.

Send information about a monthly draft from my (our) checking account.

Building Fund

I (we) will also give $_____ each _____ to the Building Fund.

Giving will be a priority in my (our) life, growing to include the following:

Giving will be the greatest joy in life. If I miss a week, I (we) will give twice as much the next week to keep faith with this commitment. I (we) will move closer to tithing (giving 10%) each year. The check to the church will be the first one I (we) write each month.

New believers and pre-Christians may struggle with a commitment to make any level of financial gift. For some new believers, this will be the first time they have given to any charity. The commitment can be as simple as "Yes, I will give $5 per week." This initial invitation is modest, but it may prove to be the first step toward a life-long journey toward a devoted life of tithing.

For those who occasionally place $1 or $5 in the offering plate, they may be ready to accept the invitation to increase that amount to $5, $10, $20, or $30. The commitment card for this week invites each individual to write in the amount of the commitment and to indicate whether the gift will come weekly, monthly, quarterly, or yearly. There is also a space where respondents have the option of indicating whether this is a ten percent tithe, or what percentage this amount represents. You may want to mention the joy of beginning a journey toward double or triple tithing.

There are two versions of the commitment card to choose from: one that only includes the church's general fund, or a second version that also includes the building fund.

Concerning the collection of money for God's people: you should do what I have directed the churches in Galatia to do. On the first day of the week, each of you should set aside whatever you can afford from what you earn so that the collection won't be delayed until I come. Then when I get there, I'll send whomever you approve to Jerusalem with letters of recommendation to bring your gift.
1 Corinthians 16:1-3 (CEB)

Financial giving is not just about the amount of the gift but the qualities of a mature giving lifestyle that include giving as the greatest joy in life, a promise to make up for missed offerings, a pledge to move toward tithing, and a determination to make the offering check the first one written each month.

This Sunday, you and the Follow-through Task Group (see Part 2 of this program guide) are invited to set up a display in the foyer to provide information about stewardship groups and activities in your church, to help people keep this week's commitments faithfully. On Ministry Celebration Sunday, the final week of the program, these groups and activities can be presented again, along with handouts and samples of follow-up resources for people to use in the weeks and months following the program. (See the CD-ROM at the back of this book, under 6. Tools and Helps: Follow-up Resources.)

Everyone should give whatever they have decided in their heart. They shouldn't give with hesitation or because of pressure. God loves a cheerful giver.
2 Corinthians 9:7 (CEB)

---

6. Service

During the sixth and final week of the program, each household is invited to climb another step in their journey toward greater commitment to Christ. This step is about service—what it is and how it can transform life. If the people of your congregation are going to have a growing personal relationship with the Lord, it will involve giving their time and "getting blisters on their hands" for Jesus.

Brothers and sisters, I don't want you to be ignorant about spiritual gifts. There are different spiritual gifts but the same Spirit; and there are different ministries and the same Lord; and there are different activities but the same God who produces all of them in everyone. A demonstration of the Spirit is given to each person for the common good.

1 Corinthians 12:1, 4-7 (CEB)

This week we invite new disciples, for the first time, to give their time in selfless service to the Lord. This is more than a simple request to volunteer for an hour a week; it is an invitation to discover the lifestyle of servanthood, and to be good stewards of time and talents. For the mature disciple, this week invites a commitment that "as long as I have breath I will serve the Lord."

The commitment card this week asks the question, "Are you ready to grow in your hands-on service to the Lord?" The list of responses is directed toward the new believer as well as the mature disciple. The responses focus in part on the frequency but also on the quality of service. Some of your people will only be ready to make one commitment, while others will be ready to make several commitments. Respondents may check as many of the following as they would like.

- No, I am not ready at this time.
- No, I am not ready yet, but I will be searching for ways that I can serve the Lord.
- Yes, I am ready to begin giving one hour each week.
- Yes, I am ready to begin giving two hours each week.
- Yes, I am ready to begin giving _____ hours each week.
- I am most interested in serving in the following ways:

_____

_____

_____

- Service will be a priority in my life, growing to include the following:

I will look for ways to give my time and strength to serve the Lord. I will serve with joy and gladness. When I feel the Lord inviting me to greater levels of sacrifice and service, I will answer, "Yes, Lord, send me."

In response to these invitations, some of your people will be ready to make only one commitment, while others will be ready to make several commitments to grow in this area of service.

New believers and pre-Christians may struggle with the invitation to serve, so they are offered a response in which they only commit to searching for ways to serve the Lord. This initial commitment is modest, but it allows people to indicate that they are open to service opportunities in the future. This may prove to be the first step on a life-long journey toward a deeply devoted life of service in Jesus' name.

For those who occasionally or sporadically serve, they may be ready to commit to one hour each week of service. This commitment is in harmony with the level of weekly expectation in many congregations: one hour of worship, one hour of small groups, and one hour of service. They may choose in some cases to serve two or more hours each week.

Those willing to be more specific may want to indicate in what areas or ministries they are willing to serve. This invitation allows you to highlight a wide variety of service opportunities you may already have in place, ranging from one-time to short-term to long-term commitments across a wide variety of skill levels. This is also an opportunity to highlight major service opportunities such as foreign mission trips and week-long mission work camps.

The final response listed focuses on quality rather than quantity of mature service, including devoting time and strength to serve the Lord, serving with joy and gladness, and enthusiasm in answering God's call to serve.

Then he will say to those on his left, "Get away from me, you who will receive terrible things. Go into the unending fire that has been prepared for the devil and his angels. I was hungry and you didn't give me food to eat. I was thirsty and you didn't give me anything to drink. I was a stranger and you didn't welcome me. I was naked and you didn't give me clothes to wear. I was sick and in prison, and you didn't visit me." Then they will reply, "Lord, when did we see you hungry or thirsty or a stranger or naked or sick or in prison and didn't do anything to help you?" Then he will answer, "I assure you that when you haven't done it for one of the least of these, you haven't done it for me."

Matthew 25:41-45 (CEB)

The work of the Follow-through Task Group (see Part 2 of this program guide) is critical for this step. The group is asked to present and clarify the wide variety of volunteer and service opportunities that were presented during the previous weeks of the program and to make that list available for those considering service commitments. In addition, this would be a good time to remind people of the small groups at your church, which provide an ideal setting for committing to Christ.

This is not the week for "interest inventories" to be distributed. Rather, any list provided should consist of actual ministry opportunities in which individuals can quickly and readily be involved. Don't suggest ministries that your church hasn't already established. Also, don't list areas that are already operating with sufficient or excess volunteers. When drawing up your list of service opportunities, make sure all the ministries listed need help and are ready to respond. It is counterproductive to ask for people's help with a particular ministry if there isn't a current need for their service.

As part of Ministry Celebration Sunday, the Follow-through Task Group will want to set up a display table with lists and samples of resources that people can use to delve more deeply into all the program themes. A good list of resources can be found on the CD-ROM at the back of this book, under 6. Tools and Helps: Follow-up Resources.

* * *

What is the spiritual journey we are inviting others to begin? What are the marks of Christian discipleship?

The answer begins, first and foremost, with a saving relationship with Jesus Christ; it is followed and supported by a growing commitment to prayer, Bible reading, worship, witness, financial giving, and service. These six invitational steps are not ways to earn salvation but rather steps toward a generous life in response to salvation already received from Christ. This is what Committed to Christ is all about.

4.
WORSHIP AND SERMONS

One key to a fruitful and successful Committed to Christ program is the individual responsibility that the Steward and Celebration Team members are willing and able to take on. (See Part 2. Using the Program: Roles, Teams, and Functions.)

A second crucial element is worship. Worship is the primary opportunity to reach, inspire, and invite the most people in your church family to climb at least one step in their commitment to Christ.

To meet this goal, all the staff members and volunteers involved in worship need to begin well in advance to coordinate their work so as to offer the highest levels of excellence in every facet of worship during the program. As described in the previous section, the worship themes during the program are:

- Introduction. Commitment to Christ
- Week 1. Prayer
- Week 2. Bible reading
- Week 3. Worship
- Week 4. Witness
- Week 5. Financial giving
- Week 6. Service

Worship Elements

All the elements of worship (music, prayers, liturgy, graphics, sermon) should support the theme for that particular day. These activities should be designed to encourage a desire to begin or re-engage in the process of becoming a deeply devoted disciple of Jesus Christ.

When worshipers enter the sanctuary, they should find in their chairs a copy of the Six-step Brochure, along with that Sunday's commitment card.

The pastor's Scripture and sermon will focus specifically on inviting each individual to higher levels of a commitment to Christ in each of the areas of discipleship.

Personal testimony will be included. Each Sunday, a different church member will take two minutes to give a personal testimony in worship centering on the particular area of discipleship. These are not to be "mini-sermons" or Bible lessons but brief, moving, personal testimonies. (See Appendix C: Samples and Forms, as well as the CD-ROM at the back of this book: Tools and Helps > You've Been Asked to Share a Personal Testimony.)

Each Sunday the congregation will be invited to place that week's commitment card in the Covenant Box. By giving this invitation every Sunday instead of only on the last Sunday, more of the occasional attenders will be encouraged to participate.

Week by Week

The foundation is laid for a fruitful Committed to Christ program on the introductory Sunday. Some churches extend this introduction and preparation to the three or four worship services before the six weeks begin.

During the introductory week or weeks, the worship, including sermons, can begin to lay a foundation for the program by presenting invitational themes. Sermon starters are included in Appendix A. You are welcome to use these sermon starters to develop sermons of your own.

Whatever sermons you choose, the themes can be presented under the umbrella of the series title Committed to Christ. If you decide to extend the introductory Sunday, within this introductory series the sermon or sermons might include themes such as:

- "Are You Entirely Sanctified" (Mark 12:29-31)
- "Let's Live Fruitfully" (Galatians 5:16-26)
- "Shine Brightly for Christ" (Philippians 2:12-18)
- "Run With Endurance" or "Keeping Your Eyes on Jesus" (Hebrews 12:1-2)
- "Walk Worthy of Your Calling" (Ephesians 4:1-5)
- "Are You Pressing Toward the Goal?" (Philippians 3:12-21)
- "Preparing for the Harvest" (Galatians 6:7-10)
- "The Great Invitation" or "Choose Today Whom You Will Serve" (Joshua 24:14-15).

During the six weeks of the program itself, worship and sermons should follow the six themes in order. By always using the umbrella title Committed to Christ, you'll be able to take full advantage of the logo, graphics, banner, poster, flyers, and other themed materials provided on the CD-ROM at the back of this book, under Brochure, Banner, and Graphics.

During the introductory period and the six-week program itself, the elements of worship, including sermons, should be invitational more than educational. At the end of each sermon, the desired response is a commitment to climb one or more steps in that particular area of discipleship. To put it another way, the desired response is "I will take the step with God's help" rather than "I didn't know that."

For example, during the week when prayer is the theme, the desired response is not for the congregation to know more about prayer, but rather for individuals in the congregation to commit to climbing one or more steps in their personal prayer life. Similarly, during the week when worship attendance is the theme, the desired response is not for the congregation to know more about worship but rather for individuals in the congregation to commit to climbing one or more steps in worship attendance. And of course, during the week when financial giving is the theme, the desired response is not for the congregation to know more about the church budget, but rather for individuals in the congregation to commit to climbing one or more steps closer to the biblical minimum standard of a 10% tithe.

As always, these are not steps toward earning one's salvation, but rather steps toward a generous life in response to salvation already received from Christ.

To help you coordinate the worship elements and present the themes graphically, we have prepared a DVD (available separately or in the Committed to Christ Kit) containing video loops and sermon lead-ins that will be useful in building a consistent visual theme during worship.

In addition, the kit contains short devotions and prayers, suitable for use on social media, on a bonus CD-ROM: *Tweets, Posts, and Prayers.* The worship each week can build on the devotional life of the congregation from the prior week by echoing elements or phrases from these devotions and prayers in the gathered worship services.

Making It Work

- Plan worship and sermons well in advance.
- Consider allowing extra time between the Introductory Sunday and Week 1, so the congregation can prepare and focus.
- Coordinate worship elements to support the theme: music, prayers, liturgy, graphics, sermon.
- Choose dynamic speakers to offer personal testimonies.
- Plan elements of worship to be invitational (doing) more than educational (knowing).

5.
SMALL GROUPS

The small groups in your congregation (Sunday school classes, home groups, or midweek groups) provide the perfect setting for taking the program's invitational possibilities to the next level. Congregations are encouraged to notify all their small groups and invite them to study and reflect on the six themes during Committed to Christ, in harmony with the worship theme schedule.

For the small groups that accept this invitation, Committed to Christ carries the potential of planting transformational seeds in every household and in the church itself. Just imagine:

- Your congregation striving, step by step, to take a faithful journey toward becoming deeply devoted servants of the Lord.
- Small groups living and serving generously together in response to the saving grace of the Lord, not as an obligation but in joyous response.
- This balanced, generous life arising out of each small group's commitment to Jesus Christ, flowing through every facet of their daily lives.

To help you incorporate small groups into the program, we have provided an *Adult Readings and Study Book* for group members and a *Small Group Leader Guide* for those leading or facilitating the groups.

In some congregations, small group leaders will want to meet one or more times to review these resources and plan activities together. In other congregations, small groups are rather independent and autonomous. In the latter case, we recommend that small group leaders be contacted as soon as a decision is reached to use the program. This contact can be made through an advance e-mail or letter describing the basic themes of Committed to Christ and suggesting that their small group might appreciate the opportunity to discuss and reflect on these themes in depth during the six-week program. The e-mail or letter should also mention the *Adult Readings and Study Book* and the *Small Group Leader Guide,* and recommend that they order copies early.

In churches with consistent, coordinated curriculum in all adult small groups, inform leaders early about the program and resources. These small group leaders will want advance copies of these resources so they can begin to prepare.

Nontraditional Small Groups

To expand the reach of Committed to Christ, consider inviting nontraditional small groups to begin a six-week focused study.

Do you have a team that meets on Saturdays to mow the lawn, edge the sidewalks, weed the flower beds, and trim the hedges? If so, invite them to meet forty-five minutes early for six Saturdays and to use the *Adult Readings and Study Book* and the *Small Group Leader Guide* to shape discussion. This same invitation can be given to office volunteers, the church set-up and tear-down teams, youth choir, men's quartet, and band, as well as to formal administrative teams in the church, such as finance, trustees, deacons, councils, and boards. In every case, it is an invitation for the group to take their commitment to Christ and their relationships with each other to a new level and to join the rest of the congregation in a season of prayer, reflection, and commitment to grow toward becoming deeply devoted disciples of Jesus Christ.

There is another kind of small group that most congregations never think of including. I am referring to the individual households of your church. The devotional book, *Committed to Christ: 40 Devotions for a Generous Life,* is an excellent resource for families to use while reading, praying, reflecting, and discussing the commitments together. If a decision is made to encourage use in the home, copies of *40 Devotions* can be mailed to each household, along with a cover letter with ideas for use in the home. Larger churches seeking to involve every household may want to invite the heads of household to a one-time or weekly training on how to lead the discussion in the home.

Small Groups at the Pastor's Home

This is a wonderful idea from Bill Easum's monograph "The Missing Piece."[7] The idea is to divide the entire church into small groups and invite them to the pastor's home for dessert and coffee. My personal experience is that over 80% of those who attended these events not only completed the commitment cards but also increased their financial commitment to the church's general fund.

The home location for this occasion makes a difference because it communicates the pastor's personal support for the program. For cases in which the pastor's home is not available, small groups can convene in the church parlor.

Keep these meetings short—ideally, under an hour. As guests arrive, serve dessert and coffee. After a few minutes, the pastor welcomes the group and shares a personal vision for the future of the church—ten minutes or less. Next, the Steward or Stewards briefly give an overview of the program and distribute all the commitment cards (three minutes). The Lay Leader or Council Chair asks those present to "climb up one step" in each area, emphasizing that increased financial support will help make this vision become a reality. The pastor closes the time with a prayer and invites the guests to take a second helping of dessert and visit for a while.

In congregations with worship attendance under 300, it might be possible to invite every household to attend one of several coffees. In larger churches, the invitation list might be limited. You might decide to invite the Committed to Christ team to attend and ask each of them bring two additional congregational leaders (church officers, small group leaders, Sunday school class leaders, and leaders from each ministry area). In this way you'll expand the number of leaders who receive the invitation from the pastor to make advance commitments to "step up."

Making It Work

- Stress the importance of small groups during the program, because these groups are where Christian commitments take root.
- When planning small groups for the program, be sure to include both traditional groups (Sunday school, Wednesday evening) and nontraditional groups (office volunteers, choirs, church committees).
- Don't overlook individual households as small groups, which can be resourced using the devotional book.
- Consider holding small groups at the pastor's home.

6.
PRAYERS AND DEVOTIONS

One of the six steps of Committed to Christ—in fact, the first step—is an invitation to commit to prayer. The program kit contains two items that can help your congregation begin to grow in its prayer life. The first item, available in the kit or for purchase separately, is a companion devotional book, *Committed to Christ: 40 Devotions for a Generous Life,* offering one devotion per day for the duration of the program. The second item, a bonus for kit purchasers, is the CD-ROM *Tweets, Posts, and Prayers,* suitable for use with Facebook, Twitter, and other social media. Your church can send the CD-ROM devotions and prayers to the congregation before, during, and after the program or post them on the church Web site.

These resources are designed to be inspirational, educational, and invitational in nature as they help you encourage your entire congregation to engage (or re-engage) in the journey toward becoming a deeply devoted disciple of Jesus Christ. The prayers and devotions are timed to coincide with a season of preparation prior to Committed to Christ, the six weeks of the program itself, and a follow-up after the formal program is completed.

The use of this resource will help you reach your congregation in new ways, on levels beyond what worship and small groups may be able to offer.

Making It Work

- Consider giving or making available a copy of the devotional book to every household in your church.
- Be creative in your use of the ideas and materials in the devotional *CD-ROM: Tweets, Posts, and Prayers,* including Facebook, blogs, and Twitter.

7.
WHY COMMITTED TO CHRIST

Now that you've been introduced to Committed to Christ, you may be wondering why your church will want to get involved. Here are some reasons to consider, based on the experience of churches that have used the program.

- It can be a powerful invitation for every person in your congregation to enter into, or re-engage, in a journey toward becoming a deeply devoted disciple of Jesus Christ.
- It carries the potential to transform every household and the church itself.
- The "generous life" engendered by the program involves having the people of your church live and serve in the saving grace of the Lord, not as a obligation but as a joyous response. This balanced and generous life, arising out of a commitment to Jesus Christ, flows through every facet of daily living.

"You have been treated generously, so live generously."
Matthew 10:8 (*THE MESSAGE*)

- The program's holistic, six-step invitation is closer to the broad range of the Lord's high expectations for those who seek to follow faithfully. These six primary commitments are worthy of giving one's life to.

How is it different?

Committed to Christ is not your typical annual stewardship campaign, for several reasons:

- Your congregation is invited to journey together in a more holistic set of commitments than most annual stewardship campaigns, which focus almost solely on financial giving.
- The program begins by inviting your congregation to make or affirm their personal commitment to Jesus Christ.
- In response to that primary commitment to Jesus Christ, invitations are offered to take one or more steps in six additional areas of discipleship.
- Equal emphasis is placed on each area of commitment. The use of separate commitment cards (instead of a single combined card) helps to communicate the message that a range of commitments are being sought.

In many traditions, the six steps in Committed to Christ reinforce the church's basic expectations of all who seek to be faithful disciples: prayers, Bible reading, worship, service, gifts, and witness.

While the typical commitment card for other programs may have a box to check about prayer, attendance, and service, the "pledge card" goes on to ask the congregation to indicate if financial support will be weekly, monthly, quarterly, or annually in cash, by bank draft, or in final estate planning. In this way the typical annual stewardship program communicates that the "bottom line" is a financial commitment. This sends the wrong message.

In contrast to the typical program, Committed to Christ begins with an invitation to follow Jesus Christ as Lord and Savior. It then invites the congregation to respond in six areas of discipleship to the saving grace of God and thus begin a journey together toward becoming deeply devoted disciples of the Lord.

How will your congregation be enriched and changed?

Committed to Christ holds the potential of increasing the level of vital personal faith in your congregation, including such signs as regular prayer and Bible Study, consistent attendance at weekly worship, proportional giving, participation in mission opportunities, and personal faith sharing.

A recent study in one faith tradition has shown some of the benefits of having lay leadership exhibit such signs of vital personal faith. A church with leadership exhibiting these signs is 48% more likely to be a high-attendance church; 54% more likely to be a high-growth church; 30% more likely to be a high-engagement church; and 84% more likely to be a church with a high level of vitality.[8]

> *Don't just do the minimum that will get you by. Do your best. Work from the*
> *heart for your real Master, for God. . . .Keep in mind always that the ultimate*
> *Master you're serving is Christ.*
>
> Colossians 3:22-23 (*THE MESSAGE*)

Churches with a high level of vitality are rare. In the typical congregation, it seems that only a small portion of the congregation is actively engaged and striving to become faithful disciples of Jesus Christ; in contrast, the vast majority of the typical congregation seems to be more passive or lukewarm in their response. The same study cited above found that only 15% of its churches in the United States were high vitality; 49% were medium vitality; and 36% were found to have low vitality.[9]

Committed to Christ invites every household in the congregation to take at least one step in six different areas, beginning with a growing commitment to Jesus Christ. Through these six invitations, Committed to Christ lays the foundation for the vitality of your church to surge forward as commitments are made and kept. Imagine the people of your congregation becoming so engaged in the journey that they insist, like some who have used the program, on repeating Committed to Christ year after year, as they continue to step up and grow toward becoming deeply devoted disciples.

Will giving increase?

You might be wondering, "Will the strategies in Committed to Christ increase our congregation's per capita giving?" Great question. While it's true that financial giving is not the only goal of Committed to Christ, an increase in giving should certainly be one result.

In the landmark book *Money Matters: Personal Giving in American Churches*, Dean R. Hoge and his co-authors report that churches fall into three general categories regarding how they ask parishioners to contribute money.[10] The first category is called an offerings church. These churches do not hold an annual financial stewardship campaign. The parishioners are simply invited to respond to the offering plate each week. In these churches, parishioners on average give 1.5% of their income to the church.

A second category is called a *pledging church*. In these churches, the leadership prepares an annual budget. Parishioners are then asked to give financial resources to support the budget. The message is: *Your church needs money to accomplish the ministries described in our budget. Please give generously so that these ministries can be accomplished.* In pledging churches, parishioners on average give 2.9% of their income to their church—about twice as much as in churches that do not ask their parishioners to pledge.

Herb Miller, author of *New Consecration Sunday,* calls the third category a *percentage-giving church.* In these churches, instead of preparing an annual budget first and asking parishioners to support it, the church first conducts an annual stewardship campaign that asks parishioners: *What percentage of your income do you feel God is calling you to give?* Parishioners decide the percentage, translate it into a dollar amount, and write the dollar amount on a commitment card. The church then uses the total of these commitment cards, subtracting anticipated shortfall and adding anticipated loose-plate offerings, in preparing its budget. Herb Miller says that in these churches, parishioners are not asked to "pay the bills" or "support the budget"; rather, they are asked to grow spiritually, giving a percentage of their income to the work of the Lord through their congregation. In these percentage-giving churches, parishioners on average give 4.6% of their income to their church—about three times more per year than in churches that only rely on passing the offering plate.[11]

Committed to Christ invites congregations to be *percentage-giving churches,* not focusing on the church's need to meet a budget but rather on each individual's need to respond generously to the saving grace of Jesus Christ.

Best of all, they went beyond our highest hopes, for their first action was to dedicate themselves to the Lord . . .for whatever directions God might give them.
2 Corinthians 8:5 (NLT)

II.
Planning
the Program

8.
GETTING THE CHURCH INVOLVED

In order for Committed to Christ to succeed in your church, it must truly be a congregational effort, with many people involved at several different levels.

Bad Idea: The entire program will be "run" by the pastor and office assistant, with a lay figurehead willing to have letters sent over their signature.

Good Idea: The program will involve 10% to 20% of the active congregation to play some level of leadership.

The Key to Success:
This program succeeds or fails
with the level of responsibility and involvement
by the Steward(s) and the Celebration Team

Besides the pastor and church staff, congregational leadership of the program will include the following roles:

- Steward(s)
- Coordinator

- Ministry Celebration Chair
- Celebration Team, including task groups for
  - Banner
  - Q&A
  - Covenant Box
  - Follow Through
  - Mailing Operations
  - Ministry Celebration Sunday

The pastor and office staff also will provide leadership and support. All these roles are described in more detail below, under Roles, Teams, and Functions.

9.
SELECTING AND RECRUITING

The key to the fruitfulness and success of Committed to Christ will depend on the involvement and commitment of the entire congregation, but especially on the individual responsibility level of the Steward and Celebration Team.

These must be persons of integrity who, over the years, have exhibited a commitment to the program's principles: first and foremost, accepting Jesus Christ as Lord and Savior; then praying for the church; reading the Bible daily; attending worship faithfully; serving willingly with personal time and talent; making a significant or proportional pledge to the church's general fund; and witnessing by sharing with others the good news of God's love.

The pastor will select and recruit the Steward, Coordinator, and Ministry Celebration Sunday Chair. The Steward, once chosen, will select and recruit the Celebration Team, including chairs for the remaining task groups. When selecting and recruiting for these positions, the pastor and Steward should carefully review the suggested process listed below under "Roles, Teams, and Functions."

The *Steward* should be a person held in high regard by the congregation. In addition, the Steward must be an active and enthusiastic participant with a positive vision for the church and be willing and able to communicate that enthusiasm with others. The Steward should also be one of the most generous financial supporters of the church. In some congregations, this person may already be the official Lay Leader, Council Chair, or Superintendent. In other congregations, this person may have been active for only a year or two, yet through the power of their integrity and personality will have gained the respect of the congregation.

The *Coordinator* needs to be a task-oriented self-starter with a record of taking on a project and seeing it through to successful conclusion.

The *Ministry Celebration Sunday Chair* should be a person who has positive relationships with all the individuals and groups that typically are involved with the worship services each week.

The Steward (or Stewards) will select the *Celebration Team*. The Steward will also select, from within the Celebration Team, chairs for the following task groups: Banner, Q&A, Covenant Box, Mailing, and Follow Through. (Note: the pastor already will have selected the chair of the Ministry Celebration Sunday Task Group.) The task group chairs, like the Coordinator, need to be task-oriented self-starters with a record of taking on a project and seeing it through successfully to conclusion.

A big part of the recruitment process is providing enough information about the various roles and responsibilities so that potential recruits are aware of the time and work involved and can plan their schedules accordingly. Therefore we strongly recommend that, in addition to describing the role verbally, you give the potential recruit a handout describing the responsibilities involved.

For that reason we have designed the following pages so you can photocopy (or print out from the CD-ROM) the pages for pastor, Steward, Coordinator, Celebration Team, and each of the Task Groups. We also suggest that you photocopy or print out Part 3: Implementing the Program, a short section that provides a sample schedule for the program, for team members to read and keep for reference.

For your convenience, sections of this program guide are included in PDF format on the CD-ROM at the back of this book. Please feel free to print out and distribute these sections for use in your congregation.

10.
ROLES, TEAMS, AND FUNCTIONS

Pastor

The leader of the program will be the steward (see below), but the pastor will be involved in the planning, some initial steps, and oversight. In planning, the pastor will:

- Lead or be a part of the effort to bring Committed to Christ to the church.
- Seek the Lord's guidance, strength, and Word, praying daily for the program.
- Obtain official permission from the Church Council for Committed to Christ to be this year's fall emphasis or stewardship campaign in your church.
- Be sure that your office reserves dates on the church calendar for the introductory Sunday and the six commitment Sundays that follow.
- Notify all staff departments about the dates and solicit the staff's cooperation and support of the program and its themes.
- Select and recruit the Steward, Coordinator, and Ministry Celebration Sunday Chair.

Recruiting

To begin the program, the pastor will select and recruit the Steward, Coordinator, and Ministry Celebration Sunday Chair.

When recruiting the Steward, there is no better method than a face-to-face conversation. In most cases the appointment will take place at the layperson's office or home. In preparation for the appointment, the pastor should be prepared to describe the job and answer any questions that might arise. The pastor should first briefly share a vision for the role this program will play in helping the church and congregation to step up to higher levels of discipleship; then the pastor can extend the invitation, using words similar to these:

> Betty, I need your help. I'm asking you to serve as the Steward of a program—the director, you might say, of a six-week emphasis in our church this fall. It won't be a simple responsibility. You will be putting together a Celebration Team made up of 10 to 20% of our active households. You will be inviting the team to an initial training and leading them in their primary responsibility of telephoning every household in the church, to encourage attendance on Ministry Celebration Sunday at the end of the program. During the six-week program, you will also read a brief survey report to the congregation and invite them to climb one step toward becoming a faithful disciple of Jesus Christ. You will be leading the congregation in a program that could dramatically change our church.

When recruiting the Coordinator and Ministry Celebration Sunday Chair, the pastor should follow the same procedure as outlined above for the Steward. The Coordinator needs to be a task-oriented self-starter and have a record of taking hold of a project and seeing it through to successful conclusion. The Ministry Celebration Sunday Chair should be a person who has a positive relationship with the various individuals and groups that typically coordinate the worship services each week.

Once the program is underway, the pastor will want to meet periodically with the Steward, Coordinator, Ministry Sunday Chair, and office staff to review progress; discuss any common concerns; support the survey process (see below); and confirm the calendar dates for the introductory Sunday and the six commitment Sundays that follow.

Commitment Cards

One of the pastor's main responsibilities is to present the program from the pulpit and encourage the congregation prayerfully to consider and fill out the commitment cards. There will be seven cards—one for the initial commitment to Christ and six for the commitments growing out of it: prayer, Bible reading, worship, witness, financial giving, and service.

Before the worship service each week, be sure every chair in the sanctuary is stocked with a blank copy of that week's commitment card and a sharpened pencil. (If your chairs do not have holders, place these items on the chairs themselves.) Even though the entire set of blank commitment cards will have been mailed to every household a week or two before the program begins, and even though blank commitment cards will have been placed in every worship bulletin today, you will find a significant number of worshipers who will still need help, so you should station members of the Celebration Team around the room and ask them, at the appropriate time, to stand and hand out more cards and pencils as needed.

A critical point, often missed, is the pastor's invitation for each person to mark the commitment card, sign the card, and turn it in. Note that this process will add about five to seven minutes to your worship service. Therefore, we suggest that other elements of the service be adjusted accordingly, or be prepared for the worship service to last five to seven minutes longer than usual.

You cannot move through this process quickly in worship or assume that everyone will know what to do. For this reason we strongly suggest that, on the introductory Sunday and each of the six Sundays that follow, you include the following process near the end of each sermon. *We know from past experience with the program that if you fail to follow this suggestion, the number of responses will be reduced by 25% to 50%.*

Here is the process, including our suggestions for the pastor's words and actions:

I invite everyone to look at today's commitment card.
> *Hold up one of the cards.*
You can see the various commitments listed.
> *Actually read the card aloud. Don't assume they will read it silently.*
As you can see, the first level of commitment is _____.
The second commitment is _____.
The third commitment is _____.
The fourth commitment is _____.
The fifth commitment is _____. (And so on.)
> *Then slowly, clearly, and distinctly say the following:*

I don't know what level your commitment has been, but I know what level my commitment has been. Today we are all invited to take one step in a new commitment. Please take the pencil there in front of you, and let's fill out and sign that card now.

> *Here it is critical that you lead by example. Pause, take a moment to look at your card, and sign it while everyone is watching. Then wait for the worshipers to fill out their own cards. If you are willing, you might consider making your own level of commitment known. This can serve as a powerful leadership witness.*

As we sing the closing hymn now (or as we listen to the choir), you are invited to bring your card to the front (or move to one of the stations) and place your card in the locked covenant box as a sign of your commitment to climb one step in the coming year.

Note: The reference here to a locked box and the visible brass lock on the box it-self, which will emphasize that each individual commitment is confidential.

In addition to presenting the commitment cards, the pastor should preach on the topic that matches the commitment card for that particular Sunday: commitment to Jesus Christ, prayer, Bible reading, worship, witness, financial giving, or service. Sermon ideas are included in Appendix A: Sermons Starters.

The final week, on Ministry Celebration Sunday, the pastor or Steward will announce the totals from the commitment cards received on the previous Sundays.

After the program, the pastor will want to send thank you letters to the Steward, Coordinator, and Celebration Team members.

Following Up

In the weeks and months following the program, you'll want to remind the congregation of the commitments they have made, as individuals and as a church. Here are some effective ways to do that.

- Remind the Q&A Task Group to keep the Committed to Christ table set up in the lobby for the first week following the program. During worship that Sunday, remind the congregation about the table, saying something like this:

In the lobby after worship, you will find the Committed to Christ table, with copies of the seven commitment cards we have been looking at these past forty days. If you missed worship recently, be sure and stop by the table and complete the commitment cards you missed, so you can join with the rest of the congregation in this journey toward becoming deeply devoted disciples of Jesus Christ. On the table you'll also find a covenant box to receive your cards.

- About once a month after completion of the program, refer to the commitment cards during your sermon. Hold up one of the cards and talk about it. You'll find it especially easy to remind the congregation about the commitment cards if you prominently display a covenant box at the front of the sanctuary. Every month or two, if you are preaching a sermon that relates to one of the seven commitments, walk over to the covenant box, put your hand on it, and say something like this:

Some of you remember that, during this past year, _____ of us put commitment cards in this box. In doing so, we made a commitment to take one or more steps in our commitment to Christ. How is that going for you? Are you keeping the commitment? My friends, this is a good week to start, or to continue. Maybe you've been on-again and off-again during the past few weeks—I understand. This week is going to be different. We are going to take that step together. Are you ready?

- Sometime after the end of the program, consider a sermon directed toward those who made commitments but have not yet tried to meet them. Such a sermon, perhaps titled "A Perfect-fitting Yoke," might be based on Jesus' words of comfort and reassurance in Matthew 11:28-30. You might begin by saying something like this:

Is this you? You looked over the commitment cards. You thought to yourself, "I can do that!" You checked all the right boxes on the cards. Now, a few weeks later, you look up and wonder what happened to all those promises. If that's your story, you're learning how hard it is to change old habits; and how hard it is to sacrifice. I have good news for you: It doesn't stay hard; it gets easier. Listen to these words of our Lord Jesus: (Read Scripture.) The good news is this: As you begin to move in harmony with the Lord, it gets easier!

New Members

Some churches may choose to continue the Committed to Christ program beyond the first year. It can be especially effective with new members. In that case, when speaking to the new members' class the pastor might say something like this:

This church is a high-expectation church. We expect our members to have a personal commitment to Jesus Christ as their Lord and Savior; to pray every day; to read the Bible daily; to be in worship every Sunday they are physically able; to give at least one hour a week of hands-on service in Jesus' name; to support the church financially, growing to the biblical minimum standard of the 10% tithe; and to invite others to worship with them.

If you are looking for a church to join but only attend on Christmas and Easter, this may not be the church for you. Each of our members has been invited on a journey toward faithful Christian discipleship, climbing one step closer each year. We do that with this set of commitment cards. Let's take a look at each of these cards....

If you decide to make our church your home, we invite you to fill out these cards and hand them to me on the Sunday when you come to the front.

In one church that implemented Committed to Christ, prospective new members were introduced to the concept of the cards and given a return envelope with a label on the front of the envelope, stating: "On the Sunday you decide to join, hand this sealed envelope to the pastor, containing the yellow information card and all the signed commitment cards." The church reported that 95% of their new members (averaging 48 households a year) handed the pastor all seven signed commitment cards when they came to the front to join.

The church also included a yellow new member information card with blanks for full name, nickname, age, employment, grade in school, interests, and hobbies. When the family came to the front, the pastor opened the envelope and used the yellow card to introduce them to the congregation. The church office used the yellow card to complete membership records and to write an article for the church's weekly e-mailed newsletter.

On the rare occasion when a family forgot to bring the sealed envelope, the church office staff called them first thing on Monday and asked, "Can you drop that envelope by the office today? We need those cards for our records." In every case, in response to this call, the set of cards was delivered to the church office within two days.

Pastor's Task List

June

- Begin with prayer for the fruitfulness of the Committed to Christ: Six Steps to a Generous Life program.
- Obtain from your local church's governing body official permission to make Committed to Christ the year's fall emphasis.
- Work with the office staff to set dates on the church calendar for the introductory Sunday and the six Sundays that follow. Consider scheduling the introductory Sunday a few weeks in advance of the six-week program, to allow time for the congregation to prepare and focus on the program.
- Meet with local church staff to review the program process carefully, discuss any concerns, obtain their support, and confirm dates on their calendars.
- Decide if you are going to hold the optional late September small group gatherings in the pastor's home. (See "Small Groups at the Pastor's Home" in Part 1: Small Groups.)
- Prayerfully recruit the Steward(s), Coordinator, and Ministry Celebration Sunday Chair. (For help in choosing the right people for these key positions, see Part 2: Selecting and Recruiting.) Larger churches might want to have a sixth grader and a youth to be the Stewards of their age levels.

July/August

- Engage the congregation's communication networks to announce the program and educate the congregation concerning its theme and the six commitments that are part of that theme.
- To promote the program and introduce it to your congregation, consider mailing to every household a copy of the little preview book, *Six Steps to a Generous Life: Living Your Commitment to Christ,* along with an invitational letter.
- Invite all small groups in the church to use the *Adult Readings and Study Book* and

the *Small Group Leader Guide* during the program.

- Order additional copies as needed of the *Program Guide, Adult Readings and Study Book,* and *Small Group Leader Guide.* (Portions of the *Program Guide* are provided in PDF format on the CD-ROM at the back of this book, from which additional copies can be printed out for use in your congregation.)

- Meet with the Steward, Coordinator, Ministry Celebration Sunday Chair, and office staff to review the program process carefully, discuss any concerns, and confirm dates on the church calendar. Decide together if Ministry Celebration Sunday will include a luncheon. (See Appendix B: Optional Celebration Luncheon.)

- Work with the Steward and Coordinator to plan the survey process, to take place on four consecutive Sundays in August. The entire survey process should be complete at least a week or two before the introductory Sunday of the program.

- Consider holding advance small groups in the pastor's home during September. (See "Small Groups at the Pastor's Home" in Part 1: Small Groups.)

September

- Work with the Steward to recruit the lay witnesses needed in worship for the introductory Sunday and each of the six Sundays that follow. As a guide for you and the lay witnesses, see "You've Been Asked to Share a Personal Testimony" in Appendix C: Samples and Forms, as well as on the CD-ROM > Tools and Helps.

- Review with office staff the mail and printing schedule for these six weeks.

- Call the Steward to offer support and answer questions.

- Attend the Celebration Team meeting. To help ensure greater participation, you may offer identical meetings on two consecutive evenings.

- To help prepare your congregation for the first Sunday of the program (Week 1. Prayer), consider sending a copy to every household of the devotional book, *Committed to Christ: 40 Devotions for a Generous Life.*

October/November

- Preach on the particular theme each Sunday that matches that Sunday's commitment card. Sermon starters are provided in Appendix A.

- Make your personal commitment on the cards, then sign and place them on the altar.

- Invite the congregation to fill out and hand in commitment cards. (See "Commitment Cards," above, to find detailed instructions for doing this.)

- Make arrangements for a report of the survey results to be given on the introductory Sunday and each of the six Sundays that follow. (See Appendix C: Samples and Forms, as well as "Survey" on the CD-ROM at the back of this book.)

Mid- to Late November

- Send a thank you note to the Steward.
- Send a thank you note to all the giving households in the church. Follow-up thank you letters will be sent to each household monthly or bi-monthly with the individual giving record attached. (See Appendix C: Samples and Forms, as well as "Letters" on the CD-ROM at the back of this book.)
- Work with the Follow-through Task Group to design and implement a system for welcoming potential and new members of the church. (See "Follow-through Task Group," below.)

Steward

The Steward is the lay leader of the entire program. This person must be an active and enthusiastic participant with a vision for the church. The Steward needs to have the trust and respect of the congregation and be willing and able to communicate that enthusiasm to others in the church. The Steward should also be one of the church's most generous financial supporters.

In some congregations, this person may already be the official Lay Leader, Council Chair, or Superintendent. In other congregations, the person may have been active for only a year or two, yet through the power of their integrity and personality they have gained the respect of the congregation.

Responsibilities

The Steward must make a personal commitment to
- accept Jesus Christ as Lord and Savior
- pray daily for the Church
- read the Bible
- attend worship faithfully
- witness and share the good news of God's love with others
- make a significant or proportional pledge to the general fund of the church
- serve willingly with time and talent

Some churches, because of size, may want to have more than one Steward. Here is a guide that may be helpful as you decide how many Stewards to have.

- Worship attendance less than 200: 1 Steward
- Worship attendance 200 to 300: 2 Stewards

- Worship attendance 300 to 500: 3 Stewards
- Worship attendance 500 and up: 4 Stewards

One of the Steward's most important responsibilities is the selection and recruitment of the Celebration Team. Information about that responsibility can be found under Steward's Task List (below). For more detail about all the Steward's responsibilities and how they relate to the responsibilities of other program leaders, see Part 3: Implementing the Program.

Steward's Task List

June
- Agree to serve as Steward for Committed to Christ.

July
- Meet with the pastor, Coordinator, Ministry Celebration Sunday Chair, and office staff to review the program process carefully, discuss any concerns, and confirm dates on the church calendar. Decide together if Ministry Celebration Sunday will include a luncheon. (See Appendix B: Optional Celebration Luncheon.)
- Work with the pastor and Coordinator to plan the survey process, to take place on four consecutive Sundays in August.

August
- Work with Coordinator to put the confidential survey in every seat each Sunday of this entire month. Receive results from the Coordinator and report to the Congregation during worship. The survey process should be completed at least a week or two before the introductory Sunday of Committed to Christ. (See Appendix C: Samples and Forms, as well as "Survey" on the CD-ROM at the back of this book.)
- Select dates, times, and locations for the two Celebration Team training events: (1) for fellowship and overview of the program, held on two consecutive evenings sometime in mid- to late September; and (2) on the fifth Sunday of the program, for organizing the calling campaign to encourage the congregation to attend Celebration Sunday, the sixth and final Sunday of the program.
- Coordinating with the pastor, compile a list of potential Celebration Team members and then give the names to the church office. You will be inviting 10 to 20% of the church households to be on the Celebration Team. But sure to include a broad base of church households representing every small group and age level within the church. The Financial Secretary can help you ensure that the most generous financial givers are included in your Celebration Team. The Youth Minister may have suggestions of several youth to serve on the Celebration Team.

- The office will send an invitational letter to these potential Celebration Team members, including dates of the two training sessions. About ten days later, the Steward and Coordinator will telephone those who have not yet confirmed with the office. (See the sample letter in Appendix C: Samples and Forms, and on the CD-ROM at the back of this book.) When the Celebration Team membership is complete, send the final list of names to the church office and pastor.
- Recruit the lay witnesses (after they are approved by the pastor) who will be needed in worship for the introductory Sunday and each of the six Sundays that follow. Refer to the document "You've Been Asked to Share a Personal Testimony." (See Appendix C: Samples and Forms, as well as the CD-ROM at the back of this book.) If your church has the technology available, these testimonies are often better if they are recorded on video, edited, and shown on screens during worship. After worship these videos can be posted on the church Web site and distributed through social media.
- Review with Coordinator and office staff the mailing and printing schedule for the program.

September
- Finalize the Celebration Team and divide it into six task groups: Banner, Q&A, Covenant Box, Follow Through, Mailing, and Ministry Celebration Sunday.
- Host the first training session for the Celebration Team, to be held on the two consecutive evenings in mid- to late September that you previously selected. The church will send a reminder letter ten days before the training, and you should also e-mail or telephone your Celebration Team a few days before this training event to remind them and encourage their attendance.
- For a detailed list of the Steward's responsibilities as host of the first training session, see Part 3: Training.
- Working with the Coordinator and pastor, be sure that the various Task Groups are functioning.

October/November
- Report each Sunday on program progress and survey results. (Detailed instructions for reporting survey results are given in Part 3: Survey.)
- Introduce a different church member each Sunday to give a personal testimony in worship, centering on the area of discipleship that is the theme for the week.
- Working with the Coordinator and pastor, be sure that the various Task Groups (Ban-

ner, Q&A, Covenant Box, Follow-through, Mailing Operations, and Ministry Celebration Sunday) are functioning.

- Immediately after the fourth Sunday of the program, have the office send reminders to the Celebration Team to gather briefly on the fifth Sunday (or the following Monday) for a second training session, to select households they will be calling that week.

- If a decision has been made to have a luncheon on Ministry Celebration Sunday, adjust the content of the reminder letter and be prepared to give luncheon assignments at this training session. You will also need to adjust the content of the phone calls to secure reservations for the luncheon.

- On the fifth Sunday evening the Celebration Team will meet. Detailed instructions for this second training session are given in Part 3: Training.

- As Steward, you will follow up with your Celebration Team members individually by phone at least once early in the week when they will be making their phone calls. (The Coordinator may assist in making these phone contacts.) Offer your enthusiastic support, and assistance if needed, to the team members as they fulfill their duties and make their assigned phone calls that week. Remind them to complete their telephone calls and report back to you by Thursday evening before Ministry Celebration Sunday. Also, remind them to let you know any pastoral concerns that need to be relayed to the church office (such as illness, death, and personal issues).

Mid- to Late November
- Announce totals from the commitment cards received on the Sundays of the program.

- Send a thank you letter to the Celebration Team members.

- Working with the Coordinator and pastor, be sure the Follow-through Task Group is organized and functioning.

Coordinator (will work closely with office staff)

The Coordinator should be a task- and detail-oriented person who will keep everyone on schedule and assist with the telephone. The Coordinator, like the other program leaders, will seek the Lord's guidance, strength, and Word for this task, praying daily for the Steward, the Celebration Committee, the Church Council, and the whole church fellowship.

Responsibilities
The Coordinator will post all the program events on the church calendar and arrange the

printing schedule for letterhead, commitment cards, and other program needs as they arise.

After confirming with the pastor, the Coordinator will direct the church office to order additional copies of this *Committed to Christ Program Guide* as needed. (Portions of the *Program Guide* in PDF format can be found on the CD-ROM at the back of this book, and copies may be printed out for the Celebration Team and others in your congregation.) The office should also order enough copies of the *Adult Readings and Study Book* for each member of your small groups (Sunday school, home-based, or mid-week), as well as a *Small Group Leader Guide* for each group leader. The Coordinator may also decide to order copies of either the little preview book, *Six Steps to a Generous Life: Living Your Commitment to Christ,* and send one to each household with a cover letter from the pastor to introduce the program; or, copies of the devotional book, *Committed to Christ: 40 Devotions for a Generous Life,* to lead into and set the tone for the first week of the program.

In general, the Coordinator is in charge of all program logistics, working with the office staff and various teams to organize and implement the following efforts and others. Most of the documents needed, and many others, can be found on the CD-ROM at the back of this book.

- Print and hand out copies of the confidential survey. Tally the survey results for use by the Steward in reporting to the congregation during worship.
- Send the Six-step Brochure and commitment cards to the printer.
- Send invitation letters to potential Celebration Team members. The Steward will provide a list of names.
- Send reminder e-mails about team meetings.

The Coordinator should work with the church office to take advantage of the Committed to Christ CD-ROM *Tweets, Posts, and Prayers* in the *Committed to Christ Kit* that includes prayers and devotions for use on social media, making sure to promote this resource, as well as the entire program, on the church Web site.

Coordinator's Task List

June

- Agree to serve as Coordinator for Committed to Christ.

July

- Meet with the pastor, Steward, Ministry Celebration Sunday Chair, and office staff to review the program process carefully, discuss any concerns, and confirm dates on the church calendar. Decide together if Ministry Celebration Sunday will include a luncheon.
- Work with the pastor and Steward to plan the survey process, to take place on four

consecutive Sundays in August.

- Begin, with the office staff, to handle the logistics and support of the program. Put all Committed to Christ events on the church calendar, and arrange printing as needed.
- After confirming with the pastor, have the church office order (or print out from the CD-ROM at the back of this book) multiple copies of this program guide for the Steward (or Stewards), Coordinator, and six Task Group Chairs; enough copies of the *Adult Readings and Study Book* for each member of your small study groups (Sunday School, home based, or mid-week); and a *Small Group Leader Guide* for each group leader. You may also decide to order copies of the little preview book, *Six Steps to a Generous Life: Living Your Commitment to Christ,* and the devotional book, *Committed to Christ: 40 Devotions for a Generous Life.*
- Work with the church office to take advantage of the CD-ROM *Tweets, Posts, and Prayers,* which includes suggested Twitter prayers and devotions for your church's Web site or and for use on social media during the weeks of the program.

August

- Receive a list of potential Celebration Team members from the Steward. Work with office staff to send an invitational letter. About ten days later, the Steward and Coordinator will telephone those who have not yet confirmed with the office.
- Review with Steward and office staff the mailing and printing schedule for the program.
- If the pastor has decided to hold the optional late-September small group gatherings in the pastor's home, see that invitation letters are sent out. (See "Small Groups at the Pastor's Home" in Part 1: Small Groups.)
- Work with the Steward to put the confidential survey in every seat each Sunday of this entire month. Tally the survey results for use by the Steward in reporting to the Congregation during worship on each of the six Sundays of October/November.

September

- In early September, send the Six-step Brochure and commitment cards to the printer.
- Work with office staff to mail an introductory letter, the Six-step Brochure, and seven commitment cards to the entire church family. This package may also include, for each household, a copy of the little preview book, *Six Steps to a Generous Life: Living Your Commitment to Christ*; or copies of the devotional book, *Committed to Christ: 40 Devotions for a Generous Life.* Depending on church size, consider having the Mailing task force hand-address these packages. For out-of-town members, it would be wise to include a self-addressed return envelope with postage attached.

- Coordinating with the Steward and pastor, be sure that the various Task Groups are functioning.

October/November

- Keep a running tally of the commitment cards received each week.
- In the worship bulletin, include names of those giving testimonies that Sunday.
- After the fourth Sunday, send an e-mail or postcard reminder to the Celebration Team concerning the second training session, to be held on the fifth Sunday or the following Monday.
- In preparation for the Celebration Team's phone call assignments at the second training session, attach a mailing label with phone numbers to a set of 3" x 5" cards. Include all local households related to the church. Note any special concerns you know of that the telephone caller might find helpful, such as: "Both quite ill. Will not be able to attend, but still telephone to express your concern and prayers," or "Have not attended for six months," or "Her mother has been in the hospital recently," or "His wife died last month." Consult with the pastor about pulling out cards relaying special circumstances, so they can be contacted by pastoral staff or by selected Celebration Team members trained by the pastoral staff.
- Have these 3" x 5" cards ready for distribution by the Steward. The Steward may want the office to display these on tables or on the kneeling rail for the Celebration Team members to pick up.
- Also at the second training session, be prepared to hand out pencils and copies of "Instructions for Making Ministry Celebration Sunday Contacts." (See Appendix C: Samples and Forms, as well as the CD-ROM at the back of this book.)
- Immediately after the sixth Sunday, mail the Churchwide Follow-up Letter to every household related to the church. (See letter samples; see Appendix C: Samples and Forms and the CD-ROM at the back of this book.) You could create three slightly different versions of the follow-up letter: one to households that have signed all six cards; a second version for households that missed a couple of the cards; and a third version for households that may not have signed any cards.
- About a month after the sixth Sunday, mail the Thirty-day Churchwide Follow-up Letter to the same group who received the first follow-up letter. Do not include a reply envelope or commitment cards in this letter.
- After the thirty-day letter is mailed, the Financial Secretary may also want to send a letter to those who made financial commitments, to confirm the amount of the pledge.
- Working with the Steward and the pastor, be sure the Follow-through Task Group is organized and functioning.

Celebration Team

There are a number of important roles in the Committed to Christ program, but much of the impetus and leadership for the program—and ultimately its success—will come from the Celebration Team. Don't economize on the size of the Celebration Team, or you will reduce the effectiveness of the program and the number of commitment cards received. The number of households invited to be on the Celebration Team will be determined by the size of your church. We recommend 10 to 20% of the households to be represented on the team.

The more people on the Celebration Team the greater the church's commitment to the program. Work hard to recruit a variety of households. The Celebration Team should include members of the church council, trustees, finance committee, pastor-parish relations, new households, and other leaders in the church, including members of every small group or Sunday school class. If you recruit a wife and husband, count them as one.

There are practical reasons for getting many people involved, such as making sure the number of telephone calls handled by each person does not become a burden. Also, if you choose to hold the Celebration Luncheon, having a large team insures that the food preparation, food costs, and telephone responsibilities won't be too great for any one family.

If your church is typical, you probably have a core group that is quick to join any team. Don't feel limited to this group. Use the program as an opportunity to involve a broader base of church households representing every Sunday school class and age group within the church. Folks who are already serving in many other capacities, no matter how well intentioned, may become burned out and not be as supportive as you might hope.

One group that definitely should be included on the Celebration Team is the most generous financial givers. Your church treasurer or financial secretary can give you a list of those people.

Once recruited, Celebration Team members will seek the Lord's guidance, strength, and Word and pray daily for the program, their own personal level of commitment, the Steward and the other team members, the church council, and the whole church fellowship. Team members will need to attend a training event on a Sunday or Monday evening, which will include a brief inspirational address from the pastor, an invitation to make advance leadership commitments, and information about responsibilities and celebrations.

Within the Celebration Team, you'll be assigning members to six different task groups, as described below.

Banner Task Group (works closely with the Ministry Celebration Chair)

The Banner Task Group will design and construct a banner for each of the six program themes and, if desired, for each ministry area of the church. Ministry areas might include:

children, youth, women, men, food pantry, clothing bank, after-school program, nursery, prayer groups, choirs, and mission trips. (Note that these banners are in addition to the Committed to Christ program banner that is included on the CD-ROM at the back of this book.)

Begin by determining the appropriate groupings of ministries. We have seen as few as ten and as many as sixty different banners. The contact people for each ministry should be identified and notified of the date for Ministry Celebration Sunday.

Recruit the right people to assist in the creation of banners. Most churches provide the necessary materials so there is some uniformity regarding size. Organize a banner creation workshop where groups are encouraged to come and actually make their banners with help from people gifted in arts and crafts. This will serve to increase excitement for the day and help to build relationships across the various ministry areas.

Some carpentry assistance may be needed in advance for cutting the cross bar at the top, the upright pole, and bases to hold each banner. Build one sample pole and base first, to make sure the base will be broad enough to keep the banner upright.

Resist the temptation to hire a professional artist to design and create these banners. The primary task here is to involve your people actively in the program, giving them buy-in and an opportunity to interact with others during the process. You'll probably want to schedule one or more banner "parties," at which task-group members create together.

On Ministry Celebration Sunday, the Banner Task Group will assist with the banner processional. The task group will want to meet prior to that Sunday to hold a rehearsal and walk-through. If desired, write a script that will be read during the procession describing each ministry in one or two sentences. Make sure banners will be visible throughout the sanctuary; if possible, have them displayed on the large projection screen as the procession takes place. Typically the banner procession occurs during the beginning of worship, and the banners are displayed in such a way that they surround the sanctuary during the worship service.

Q&A Task Group

Members of the Q&A Task Group will organize and set up an information table near the entrance before and after every worship service during the program. In larger churches, Q&A tables may need to be placed at multiple sites.

The table will be set up for eight Sundays—the introductory Sunday, the six Sundays of the program, and the Sunday following the program. Two members of the Q&A Task Group will be at each table to offer a smiling face, answer questions, and encourage people to pick up any of the cards. Begin by determining where the table will be located, then decide which group members will be there on which Sundays.

Having an information table will be helpful to congregants who have missed one of the Sundays. The table display will include copies of all the commitment cards and a covenant box (see below). This allows the congregation to fully participate even if they have been absent a Sunday or two during the program.

Covenant Box Task Group (works quickly to have boxes ready on time)

The commitment cards and the commitments they represent are the heart of the program. To emphasize this fact, we strongly recommend that a covenant box be constructed and placed near the altar (larger churches may need more than one box and location). As part of the worship service, the congregation will be invited forward to place their commitment cards in the covenant box. An additional covenant box or boxes will be needed at each information table.

A group within the Celebration Team will form a Covenant Box Task Group to construct one or more wooden covenant boxes. The boxes should be about 8" x 14" and 6" tall, with a slot on the long side, or cross-shaped slot, in the top. The box should have a hinged lid, with a small visible brass lock to emphasize the fact that all commitments are confidential. Photos of three sample covenant box designs can be found on the CD-ROM at the back of this book under 8. Responsibilities and Task Lists: Covenant Box Task Group.

Follow-through Task Group

Prior to the first Sunday, this group will carefully review the wording of the commitment cards and determine which cards will need follow-through on each of the six Sundays and at the end of the six weeks.

For example, on the card for commitment to Jesus Christ, the pastoral staff must personally follow up if someone checks "Yes, today, for the first time, I accept Jesus Christ as my Savior." There are other follow through possibilities, too.

The Follow-through Task Group may want to consider setting up small groups related to several of the commitment cards. For example, on the Sunday of prayer commitment the group could organize a short-term class called "Learning How to Pray." On the Sunday of financial giving commitment, the group could have a class called "Managing Your Finances." On the Sunday of commitment to Bible reading, the class could be "Get Acquainted With the Bible." On the Sunday of commitment to witness, it could be "How to Witness and Share Your Faith."

To follow through on the Sunday of prayer commitment, this group might want to make available copies of the devotional book, *Committed to Christ: 40 Devotions for a Generous*

Life, or share the Committed to Christ CD-ROM *Tweets, Posts, and Prayers*, which comes in the kit.

For Ministry Celebration Sunday, which takes place on the sixth and final week of the program, the Follow-through Task Group may want to consider setting up a resource or book table in the foyer. Group the selections by subject, according to the six commitment-card topics. Alternatively, the resource tables could focus on the single theme each week. (For resource suggestions, see 6. Tools and Helps: Follow-up Resources, on the CD-ROM at the back of this book.)

The Follow-through Task Group might decide to organize a Ministry Fair on the sixth and final Sunday, with booths representing each of the ministry areas and lists of opportunities to volunteer or serve in that ministry. Be aware that the Ministry Fair, as well as the commitment cards themselves, should not include "interest inventories" for prospective ministries. Rather, any list provided should only include ministry opportunities that already exist, in which individuals could quickly and readily become involved. Also, ministries should not be listed that are closed to additional people or don't need help. The last thing you'll want to hear is complaints such as: "I volunteered to help in the nursery, but no one ever called me"; or, "I volunteered to be a Trustee, but they would not let me serve." With these issues in mind, the Follow-through Task Group needs to be careful in preparing the list of possible service opportunities.

Mailing Task Group (works with the Coordinator)

This task group will physically help with labeling, folding, and inserting the commitment cards for the two churchwide letters. Prior to each of the six Sundays, they may also be asked to place the Six-step Brochure on every chair along with that Sunday's commitment card. In churches with multiple worship services, this team may be asked to reset the brochures and cards between services.

The Mailing Task Group may also be asked to hand-address envelopes for the churchwide mailer instead of using a stick-on label. In the age of e-mail, a hand-addressed envelope greatly increases the chances of being opened and communicates that the contents contain important information. If you decide to hand-address, the Mailing Task Group could host "addressing parties" and invite Sunday school classes and other small groups to attend and help. One great advantage of having such parties is that they will tend to expand the number of households who feel included in making the program happen.

Begin and end each mailing party with prayer and a brief overview of Committed to Christ (perhaps five minutes). It is not unusual for participants to respond the way one couple did: "As we drove home that evening, it dawned on us for the first time that we needed to carefully review the commitment cards and to take our commitment seriously. It was the beginning of a new step for us as a family."

Resist the temptation to hire the local print and copy shop to handle the mailing. The primary task here is to involve your people actively in the program, giving the opportunity to invest in the program and interact with others during the process.

Ministry Celebration Sunday Task Group (works with the Banner Task Group and pastor)

Ministry Celebration Sunday is an exciting and compelling way to share ministry and service opportunities in your church and the stories of changed lives that have resulted because of them. This important event is held on the sixth Sunday of the program. The role of the Ministry Celebration Sunday task force is to ensure that the music, hospitality, and preaching should all be excellent on that Sunday. Typically it is one of the highest worship attendance Sundays of the year.

Primarily, this Sunday includes a banner processional, but your church may decide to celebrate in additional ways. You may want to have the children and youth make posters to be displayed in the entrance to worship. The making of these posters could be part of their regular Sunday morning or Sunday evening activities. The posters could show various church ministries or express what the young people like most about the church.

You could also expand Ministry Celebration Sunday by inviting each ministry area in the church to set up a display booth. In particular, ministry areas could emphasize opportunities for volunteer service. The Follow Through task group may decide to expand the day by organizing these display booths.

The task group will plan and implement Ministry Celebration Sunday. Tasks include:

- Hold rehearsals, including the Banner Task Group.
- Attend the brief training and pick up the names of households to telephone.
- Along with the entire Celebration Team, make telephone invitations on the previous Sunday, Monday, Tuesday, or Wednesday.

- Report the results of the telephone calls back to the Steward, including luncheon reservations if applicable, by Thursday at 7:00 p.m.
- Attend worship on Ministry Celebration Sunday.
- Give thanks to our Lord and Savior, Jesus Christ.

If the church decides to have a Celebration Luncheon as part of that day, the task group will also plan and implement the luncheon. Alternatively, they can set up an additional task group whose efforts will be dedicated to the luncheon.

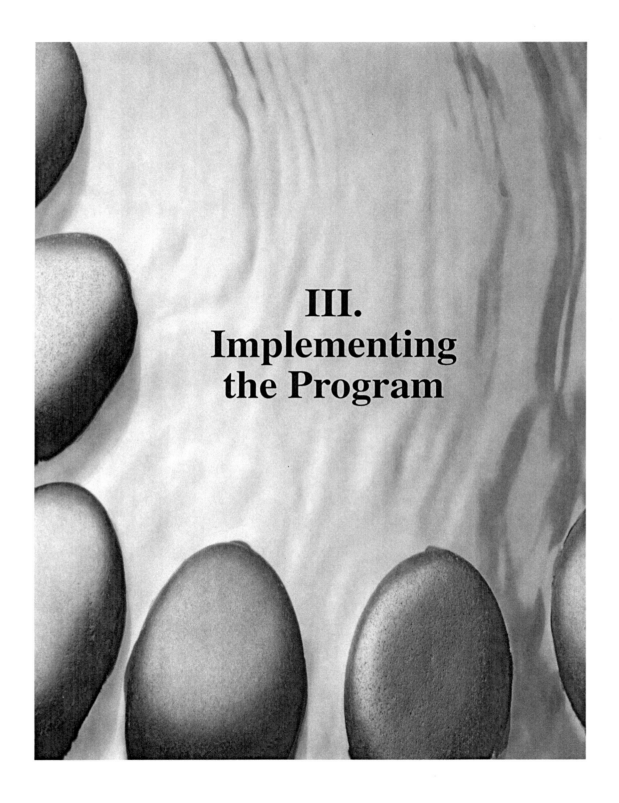

III.
Implementing
the Program

11.
INVITING THE CELEBRATION TEAM

After the pastor has selected the Steward, Coordinator, and Ministry Celebration Sunday Chair, it's time to get started.

Led by the Steward, your first task is to invite Celebration Team members. Before inviting them, you'll want to set dates for two Celebration Team training sessions, so you'll have that information when you contact potential team members.

The first training session will consist of fellowship and a program orientation. Assuming your church will hold a fall stewardship campaign, the training session will need to occur in mid- to late September. To ensure maximum attendance, consider holding the session twice, on two consecutive evenings—perhaps 6:00 p.m. on a Sunday evening and 6:00 p.m. the following Monday evening, on the third weekend of September. In some congregations, daytime gatherings work better than evenings, so you may prefer those.

The second training session, held on the fifth Sunday of the program, is to distribute contact information for the households that team members will be calling to encourage attendance the following week, on Ministry Celebration Sunday. (Detailed information about these two training sessions can be found below in "Training.")

Once you've set the training dates, you can begin contacting potential Celebration Team members. Typically, you will ask friends to be on your team. Invite people you see at church on a regular basis but do not normally socialize with; all we ask is that they be active members of the church. You might also keep in mind the value of having each small group represented on your team—Sunday school classes, women's groups, men's groups, choirs, Bible study groups, trustees, finance committee members, and so on.

It's important for the invitation to be handled in person or, more likely, by phone. Committed to Christ really begins with these initial phone calls. You are not only calling to enlist a Celebration Team member but also extending an invitation to be in fellowship with you.

The call should include a description of the program and its focus on commitments to Christ. You should explain that team members will be expected to attend two training sessions—one at the beginning of the program and one on the fifth Sunday, just before Ministry Celebration Sunday—and they may be invited to join one of several different task groups to accomplish the work of the program. In all, 10 to 20% of the congregation will be on the Celebration Team, so task group members will have sufficient support.

You will want to send a letter to your potential Celebration Team members a few days before you contact them. In larger churches you might want to include a response card or ask for e-mail or telephone responses to the church office. The Coordinator and office staff can help with this task. A sample letter can be found in Appendix C: Samples and Forms, as well as on the CD-ROM at the back of this book.

It is always more effective to follow up this invitational letter in person, perhaps before or after Sunday school or worship. Whether in person or by phone, the invitation can go something like this:

My name is _____, and I'm a member of _____ Church. I'm excited about serving as Steward for the Committed to Christ program this year. Did you get my letter about the team I'm forming?

[If the answer is no, briefly describe the program before continuing. If the answer is yes, continue by saying:]

I'd like for you to help me by serving on my team and joining us in a time of fellowship with other church members. You can pick either one of two nights—our team will meet at the church on [dates and times of the first training session]. We will also be working together in early November to telephone every household in the church, to invite them to be present for the big closing event, Ministry Celebration Sunday.

Will you help me by serving on this team?

You will encounter different responses, but most will be very positive, especially if you word your invitation in an appealing way and are sensitive to their concerns. Invite people to "help" rather than "work." Don't try to talk anyone into serving; if you do, it's likely that they won't carry out their responsibilities. You need Celebration Team members who are going to be excited about the church and serving others.

While issuing these invitations, if you discover needs requiring pastoral care, such as illness, hospitalization, or a death in the family, please relay this information back to the church office or pastor as soon as possible.

When your team is complete, send the list of names and contact information to the church office. You'll want to have your team in place by early September.

12.
TRAINING THE
CELEBRATION TEAM

As mentioned previously, there will be two training sessions for the Celebration Team. The first session, held on two different evenings before the program starts, is for fellowship and program orientation. It's an opportunity for your team to get to know each other better, to share their hopes and dreams for the church, to witness the work of Christ in their lives, *and to make their advance commitments to grow in their discipleship*. The session should be more of a relational event than a task-oriented event, but everyone should leave knowing clearly what is expected of them and inspired to make a significant response to Committed to Christ.

This first training session is so important for Celebration Team members that if they cannot attend, they will not be able to serve on the team. (This is one reason why we suggested holding the same training session on two different dates.) If a potential Celebration Team member is unable to attend the first training session, thank them for their willingness to serve and invite them to look for other ways to be a part of the program.

As a way of maximizing attendance at the first training session, some Stewards have found that a telephone call or e-mail reminder a few days before the session is helpful.

First Training Session

Set up the room in advance, placing the following on each chair: a complete set of commitment cards, including the initial commitment to Christ and the six steps following; a pencil; and a copy of the half-page sheet "Instructions for Making Celebrating Ministry

Sunday Contacts." You may also want to include a copy of the Six-Step Brochure. (See Appendix C: Samples and Forms, as well as the CD-ROM at the back of this book.)

The Steward will be the host, with the role of leading this newly formed fellowship. But the pastor and others will be involved as well.

Please open the session with prayer, followed by your personal witness about your journey with Christ and what the church means for you and your household (perhaps five minutes).

The pastor will then share a brief three-minute inspirational message and introduce the Committed to Christ program at this training event. The goal is to encourage and motivate the team.

After this brief message, the pastor will invite the Celebration Team households present to lead the congregation by making their commitments in advance, filling out the commitment to Christ card and the six additional commitment cards, then placing their cards in the Covenant Box on the altar on the first Sunday of the program.

Next, you can give a more complete overview of the program and review the calendar of events, emphasizing the team's responsibility and asking members not to miss a single Sunday during the program. Encourage team members to make an announcement about Committed to Christ in their Sunday school classes and other small groups in the church.

Introduce the task group chairpersons and distribute task list to each task group. (Reproduce task lists from CD-ROM: Responsibilities and Task Lists.)

Answer any questions your team may have. Thank each one and encourage them to pray for one another. Distribute a list of the Celebration Team members so they may continue to support each other in prayer, and contact one another, if they want to cooperate on meal preparation or other activities.

Close the training time with a prayer. Keep the entire session under one hour in length.

Second Training Session

The second training session should be held at least a week before Ministry Celebration Sunday, preferably on the evening of the fifth Sunday. The meeting's purpose is to tell the team about the telephone invitations they will be making to invite every household to come to church on Ministry Celebration Sunday.

At that meeting, the Steward or pastor will give a brief (two- or three-minute) inspirational address. Then the Steward will review the task: to telephone every household in the church family, inviting them to be present the following Sunday for Celebrating Ministry Sunday. The Steward will ask that these contacts be made Sunday, Monday, Tuesday, and Wednesday, and that team members e-mail or telephone the results back to the Steward before 7:00 p.m. on Thursday. (Keep a record of the names each team member chooses to call. This will enable you to reassign the task if they fail to make their calls.)

How do you divide up the names to call? We've found it works well to place church mailing labels (including phone numbers) on 3" x 5" cards. Spread out the cards on tables, the altar, or kneeling rail and invite team members to choose the cards of people they would like to call. Encourage them to pick five cards of people they know and five others. After this selection process, distribute any remaining cards. Then each team member should write the names they chose on the report form and leave it with you.

Should every church household be called? Households that are homebound, under hospice care, or in grief over a recent death should have their cards set aside. These households should be contacted, but they need a pastoral-care contact. These special calls may be made by trained Celebration Team members or the church pastoral staff. Other than these exceptions, every household in the area should be called. We also recommend inviting frequent worship guests. (See "Instructions for Making Ministry Celebration Sunday Contacts" in Appendix C: Samples and Forms, as well as the CD-ROM at the back of this book.)

The script for the calls is simple. You can demonstrate it at the meeting:

Hello, _____, this is _____ from _____ Church.
This week we are making telephone calls to every household related to the church, reminding everyone that this coming Sunday is Ministry Celebration Sunday. We are hoping every household will be present.
We will have great music and will celebrate all the ministries of the church.
I am looking forward to seeing you this Sunday.

If team members encounter an answering machine, instruct them to leave that same message. In some cases, leaving a voice mail can be more effective than a personal conversation. Encourage team members to avoid making phone calls past 7:30 p.m. in the evening. (That cutoff time might be adjusted depending on your particular congregation.)

If membership rolls haven't been updated in a while, you may hear something like, "I don't know why you are calling us. We attend a different church now." In that case, the caller can respond,

I didn't know that. Please excuse this call. Let me be sure I have the right information for our church office. You said that you are no longer members at our church but are members at _____ now. Can you tell me the approximate date so I can notify our office?
[Then end with:] "I am so pleased that you are active in a church. Please excuse this call.

When making this many phone calls, it will not be unusual to catch some people who are having a bad day or are angry at the church. If they start to express frustration or anger, don't argue or agree. Just wait for them to pause for a breath and offer, "I hear what you are saying. Would you like me to have the pastor call you?" They will answer, "No." At that point, quickly end the conversation by saying, "We hope you can be present this Sunday for Ministry Celebration Sunday. Good evening."

After orienting the team and rehearsing their responses to the above scenarios (typical, angry, and someone who has left church), offer your enthusiastic support and assistance if needed, to team members as they fulfill their duties and make their assigned phone calls that week. Remind them to complete their calls and report back to you by 7:00 on the Thursday evening before Ministry Celebration Sunday. Also, remind them to relay any special concerns that you learn about during calls (illness, death, personal issues) to the pastor or church office. As Steward, try to follow up with them individually by phone at least once early in the week when they will be making their calls.

At the end of the training session, answer any questions, hold a closing prayer, and collect from each person the list of people they will be calling. Keep entire session under one hour in length.

13.
SURVEY

In order to set a baseline or starting point, your church will take a survey on four consecutive Sundays in August, before the program begins. The survey asks your congregation to describe their current levels of activity and commitment in following Christ in prayer, Bible reading, worship, witness, financial giving, and service. To encourage honest answers, the survey is confidential, and the results are presented as statistics, with no names attached. Survey content and forms can be found in Appendix C: Samples and Forms, as well as the CD-ROM at the back of this book.

The surveys are distributed on the chairs or inserted in the worship bulletin during the four Sundays of August. Additional copies of the survey are handed out to all small groups and sent electronically to the congregation. Ask each person to complete the survey and place it in the offering plate the following Sunday. On the second, third, and fourth Sundays, invite those who have not yet done so to complete the survey. It will take extra paper to place a copy on each chair for four consecutive Sundays, but those extra sheets will greatly increase the number of people who participate in the survey. This is not the time to save on paper costs. The survey could also be emailed to your church contact list.

On each of the four survey Sundays, say, "On your chair today you found a confidential survey. Do not put your name on the survey. You can complete it and turn it in today, or bring it with you next Sunday."

After the survey results are tabulated, the Steward or pastor will report the findings in worship each Sunday during the program, for the particular commitment that week. The congregation will then be invited to "climb one step" in that particular area of Christian discipleship. On the introductory Sunday, for example, the announcement might be:

> Please pick up the brochure that was in your seat this morning.
>
> *Hold up a copy of the Six-Step Brochure.*
>
> This Sunday we are looking at the first and most important commitment: Will you accept Jesus Christ as your Lord and Savior?
>
> This past summer we took a confidential survey among our congregation. If you will take the pencil there in front of you, I will give you the results of the survey. You'll recall that the survey's first question was: "Have you accepted Jesus Christ as your Lord and Savior?" Next to each response or step, write the number of people in our congregation who are at that level.
>
> Next to the first step, "No, I am not ready to make a commitment," write the number 4. On the second step, "No, but maybe someday," write the number 6. On the third step, "No but I want to with all my heart," write the number 2. On the fourth step, "Yes, today for the first time," write the number 0. On the fifth step, "I have already accepted Jesus Christ," write the number 128. On the sixth step, "Yes, someday I will be ready for an even closer walk," write the number 75.
>
> *Pause, then say very clearly, slowly, and distinctly:*
>
> I do not know where you are on these stair steps, but I know which step I am on. The invitation for us today is this: Will you climb one or more steps this year?"

This survey report and invitation should take place fairly early in the worship service each Sunday, giving the congregation an introduction to the theme for the day and time to reflect on what level of commitment they are ready to make.

You will be reporting the actual numbers from the survey. The only time we would suggest altering those numbers is if only one person checked "I have never prayed" or "I never give." In that case, for pastoral reasons, I would change the number to two people, so the person won't feel like the only person in the congregation who has, for example, never prayed or never accepted Jesus Christ as the Lord and Savior.

The portion of the survey on financial giving has two sets of stairsteps (the second on percentages), so the report for that Sunday would include both sets of numbers.

14.
SAMPLE SCHEDULE

June

The pastor
- begins with prayer for the fruitfulness of Committed to Christ: Six Steps to a Generous Life;
- obtains from the church's governing body official permission to make Committed to Christ the year's fall emphasis;
- works with the office staff to set dates on the church calendar for the introductory Sunday and the six Sundays that follow;
- prayerfully recruits the Steward(s), Coordinator, and Ministry Celebration Sunday Chair.

July

The pastor
- engages the congregation's communication networks to announce the program and educate the congregation concerning its theme and the six commitments that are part of that theme;

- considers mailing a copy of the little preview book, *Six Steps to a Generous Life: Living Your Commitment to Christ,* to each household with an invitational letter in order to introduce the program;
- invites all small groups in the church to use the *Adult Readings and Study Book* and the *Small Group Leader Guide* during the program;
- orders additional copies as needed of the *Program Guide, Adult Readings and Study Book,* and *Small Group Leader Guide.* (Portions of the *Program Guide* are provided in PDF format on the CD-ROM at the back of this book, from which copies can be printed out for use in your congregation.)

The pastor, Steward, Coordinator, Ministry Celebration Sunday Chair, and office staff
- meet to review the program process carefully, discuss any concerns, and confirm dates on the church calendar;
- plan the survey process, to take place on four consecutive Sundays in August.

The Coordinator
- begins, with the office staff, to handle the logistics and support of the program.

August

The Steward
- compiles, with the pastor, a list of potential Celebration Team members and gives the names to the church office. The office will send an invitational letter. About ten days later, the Steward and Coordinator will telephone those who have not yet confirmed with the office;
- recruits the lay witnesses (after they are approved by the pastor) who will be needed in worship for the introductory Sunday and each of the six Sundays that follow. Refer to the pages "You've Been Asked to Share a Personal Testimony." (See Appendix C: Samples and Forms, as well as the CD-ROM at the back of this book.) If your church has the technology available, these testimonies are often better if they are recorded on video, edited, and shown on screens during worship. After worship these videos can be posted on the church Web site and distributed through social media;
- reviews with Coordinator and office staff the mailing and printing schedule for the program.

September

The Steward
- finalizes the Celebration Team and divides it into six task groups: Banner, Q&A, Covenant Box, Follow Through, Mailing, and Ministry Celebration Sunday.

The Celebration Team
- attends the first training session, for fellowship and planning.

The task groups
- plan and begin to carry out their functions.

The Coordinator and office staff
- mail an introductory letter and seven commitment cards to entire church family. This package may also include, for each household, a copy of the preview book, *Six Steps to a Generous Life: Living Your Commitment to Christ*.

The pastor
- calls the Steward periodically to offer support and answer questions;
- attends first training session of the Celebration Team;
- introduces the program from the pulpit during worship one or more weeks before the program begins. This is the Introductory Sunday described in Part 1. Understanding the Program: Commitment to Christ.

October/November

The church
- implements the program during six Sundays that follow the introductory Sunday:
  - First Sunday: Prayer
  - Second Sunday: Bible Reading
  - Third Sunday: Worship
  - Fourth Sunday: Witness
  - Fifth Sunday: Financial Giving
  - Sixth Sunday: Service and the Ministry Celebration

The Steward
- reports each Sunday on program progress and survey results;

- introduces a different church member each Sunday to give a personal testimony in worship centering on the area of discipleship serving as the theme that week.

The pastor
- preaches on the particular theme each Sunday that matches that Sunday's commitment card;
- invites the congregation to fill out and hand in commitment cards.

Small groups and Sunday school classes
- study the themes, week by week, using the *Adult Readings and Study Book* and the *Small Group Leader Guide.*

The Coordinator and office staff
- consider distributing or making available to each household a copy of the devotional book, *Committed to Christ: 40 Devotions for a Generous Life.*
- keep a running tally of the commitment cards received each week.

The Q&A Task Group
- provides a table at the sanctuary entrance, supplied with all the commitment cards and an additional Covenant Box, where task group members are available to answer questions about the program.

Other task groups
- continue to carry out their functions.

Mid- to Late November

The Celebration Team
- meets on the fifth Sunday of this program for the second training session, where they receive training and calling assignments;
- calls all households to invite them to Ministry Celebration Sunday;
- reports results of their calls to the Steward;
- may decide to provide a noon luncheon on Ministry Celebration Sunday for the entire congregation. At the luncheon, the pastor can give a brief inspirational address and announce a summary of the commitments made during the program.

The Banner and Ministry Celebration Sunday task groups
- rehearse Sunday activities;
- carry out plans on Sunday, including the banner procession.

The Steward
- announces totals from the commitment cards received on the Sundays of the program;
- sends a thank you letter to the Celebration Team members.

The Follow Through task group
- works with the pastor to design and implement a system for potential and new members of the church;
- implements its plan within ten days following Ministry Celebration Sunday.

The Mailing task group
- mails a follow-up letter, another set of commitment cards, a stair-step brochure, and a self-addressed return envelope to every household related to the church.

The pastor
- sends a thank you note to the Steward;
- sends a thank you note to all the giving households in the church; in addition, follow-up thank you letters will be sent to each household monthly or bi-monthly with the individual giving record attached.

APPENDIX A.
SERMON STARTERS

Matthew L. Kelley
and Bob Crossman

An important part of Committed to Christ is having the program and its goals lifted up in worship and in preaching. With that in mind, we're providing ideas for seven sermons to preach—one for the introductory Sunday on commitment to Christ and one for each of the six Sundays dealing with the six steps toward a generous life.

Of course, all pastors need to prepare their own sermons. You are free to use or not use the ideas presented here. Just keep in mind that the elements of worship, including sermons, should be invitational more than educational. Our hope is that, at the end of each sermon, the congregation makes a commitment to climb one or more steps in that particular area of discipleship. To put it another way, the desired response is "I will take this step with God's help" rather than "I didn't know that." (For more information on this approach, see Part 1: Worship and Sermons.)

However you choose to preach the seven sermons, be sure to include toward the end of the sermon an invitation for each person in the congregation to mark, sign, and turn in the commitment card. Detailed instructions for this process, including a script to follow, are given in Part 2: Pastor. Be aware that, based on our experience with the program, if you fail to follow this script and the suggested procedures that go along with it, the number of responses will be reduced by 25% to 50%.

Introductory Sunday:
"Almost Persuaded"
Acts 26:27-31 and Galatians 5:22-24

Before we begin challenging the congregation to make concrete commitments in the six steps of discipleship, we need to have them consider what it means to be a disciple of Jesus and whether they've really committed to that journey. We're not talking about commitment only in terms of accepting Christ and becoming a Christian, though that may well be the case for some people in the congregation; but about committing to making the way of Jesus their "ultimate concern," to borrow Paul Tillich's phrase.

Our text from Acts shows Paul near the end of his ministry, on trial before King Agrippa, one of Herod's sons and the Roman procurator of Judea, who was the puppet king the Romans allowed to sit on the throne. As a Roman citizen, Paul would eventually appeal to Caesar and be sent to Rome, where he would be martyred; but first, Paul was granted his request for a private audience with Agrippa. During the audience, Paul appealed to something both he and Agrippa agreed upon—the Jewish prophets—and used that appeal as an opportunity to invite Agrippa to follow Jesus. Paul's purpose was not to rebut the charges against him but simply to give a testimony to the faith that drove him. Perhaps there's a lesson for the church in Paul's actions, about not engaging in petty conflicts but keeping our focus on Christ.

While the text from Acts emphasizes the intentional nature of a commitment to follow Jesus, the text from Galatians gives a brief but very descriptive list of what a follower of Jesus looks like. While Paul's primary emphasis in this letter is on how the Holy Spirit brings these qualities out in the entire community, we can also see these things on an individual level. This descriptive list, not intended to be comprehensive (the Holy Spirit doesn't just produce these eight things!), is contrasted with another list, the "acts of the flesh," that precedes it. Through this contrast, Paul is emphasizing that we are called to focus on higher things, not short-term gain or gratification.

There are many different ways of challenging your congregation with the question of whether they are disciples and how committed they are to their discipleship. Whatever approach you take will need to be true to your own theological orientation and communicate in ways that make sense to your congregation.

I will, however, suggest two different ways to get at this question. The first way is to ponder the purpose of life. Is the goal of life simply to collect and consume as much as possible? Is it to gain wealth or fame or power or respect? In the end, all of us die, no matter how much or how little we achieve in the eyes of the world. Is there a purpose that transcends what we experience with our five senses in this lifetime? The Christian faith responds with an emphatic yes. In Christ, God has made us partners in God's redemption of all creation.

This is a purpose that goes far beyond the few years we spend here in this life. This might be a good angle to pursue if you have a lot of people in your congregation who have never made any kind of commitment to Christ.

A second way to get at the question of discipleship is to explore the list of the "fruits of the Spirit" given in the Galatians passage. Talk briefly about what each of these fruits might look like in the life of the average person in your congregation. How well does each of these fruits define our lives? If these fruits do not define us, we need to ask God to help us grow us in these areas. If people in your congregation have been Christians for a long time and yet find that one or more of these fruits are lacking in their lives, this could be what they write on today's commitment card, to use as their personal focus throughout the next six weeks.

Toward the end of the sermon, be sure to include an invitation for each person in the congregation to mark the commitment card, sign the card, and turn it in, following the script provided in Part 2: Pastor.

First Sunday:
"Are You Ready to Grow in Your Prayer Life?"
Luke 6:12-19

Last week we challenged the congregation to establish or deepen an intentional relationship with God. This week we are focusing on what is perhaps the primary means by which we engage in that relationship: prayer.

The text from Luke's gospel shows Jesus retreating to a place where he could be alone and pray all night before he made a big decision: who among his followers would assume leadership positions? The word the Bible uses for these positions is *apostles*. These leaders become major characters through the rest of Luke's gospel then take center stage in Acts, which Luke wrote as a sort of sequel to his gospel.

One of the questions people ask is why Jesus had to go away and pray so much. When we describe the Trinity, we talk about the Father and the Son being of one essence. So why did Jesus need to go talk to God if he was God?

Some folks suggest that Jesus didn't really "need" to pray, given his direct line into the mind of God, and that his doing so was merely to model faithful leadership for those twelve apostles and the many who would come after them. While that idea does appeal to the "fully God" part of Christology, it's not very satisfying to the "fully human" side. In fact, it fails to explain why Jesus, in agony, was praying in the garden of Gethsemane. Even as the divine Son of God, Jesus had the genuine need to pray.

While this Christological question is interesting, and while you should probably at least acknowledge the question in your sermon (someone in your congregation is sure to be thinking about it), spending too much time pondering what was going on inside of Jesus will distract us from the central question for today: What is the importance of prayer as it relates to being a better steward of the resources that God gives us?

One reason prayer is important is because it enables us to grow in our relationship with God. All healthy relationships have excellent patterns of communication, and prayer is how we communicate with God. Prayer is not only about talking to God and telling God our wants and needs (God already knows those things, anyway); prayer is also about listening for God speaking to us. The more essential that prayer becomes in our lives, the more we will learn to listen for the ways God speaks to us; and that listening will open us up to having our lives molded and shaped to be in harmony with God's will.

We've established that prayer is important, but we don't do our congregation any favors if we fail to spend some time addressing how we pray. There are lots of ways to approach the "how" question, and you will know what models or practices of prayer are familiar to your congregation and what they're comfortable with. Then again, maybe no one has ever really addressed the question with your church. For many in your congregation, prayer might simply be bowing their heads while someone at the front of the room makes a brief speech to God. If that's the case, this is a great opportunity to begin exploring how to pray, or to challenge your congregation with a style of prayer with which they may not be familiar.

However you choose to approach the "how" question, spend some of your sermon-preparation time by engaging in the prayer practices that you plan to introduce. You may even want to make some resources (such as Web sites, pamphlets, and classes) available to your congregation for them to further explore what it is to pray.

Close the message by asking the congregation to pull out this week's commitment card, and invite people to make a commitment to an intentional, regular prayer practice, following the script provided in Part 2: Pastor.

Second Sunday:
"Have You Read It for Yourself?"
2 Timothy 3:15-17

This week we are challenging the congregation to grow in their commitment to study the Bible on a regular basis. Last week we talked about how prayer is one of our primary means of communication with God. Build the bridge to this week's topic by emphasizing that the Holy Spirit speaks to us through Scripture, the written witness of those who came before us and share their experiences of God's transforming love.

This week's passage, from Paul's letter to his own disciple Timothy, highlights the importance of Scripture. Though Paul was speaking of the collection of texts that we call the Old Testament, we also make the same claim about the collection of New Testament texts. We believe that God inspired the writers of the biblical books and that, ever since, God has continued to use these books as a powerful means of communication and inspiration to the generations who have followed.

After establishing the significance of the Bible, you'll want to talk about why reading it regularly is important, and how we go about doing that. There are a number of ways to answer the "why" question. You could tell a story or two about people who found hope and encouragement through reading the Bible, or perhaps about someone who found a solution to a problem by reading the story of a biblical character facing similar issues. You could also refer to the lay testimony given in worship this week, describing how regular, intentional Bible study transforms lives, or you could even describe how it has transformed your own life. It would be particularly useful if these stories or testimonies showed how studying Scripture transformed ways in which people managed their resources, affected their giving to the church and other causes, and perhaps how it led them to reduce their number of possessions and look for more simplicity in life.

As in previous weeks, answering the "how" question depends greatly on your own congregational context. This is the time to invite people to participate in the various Bible-study opportunities your congregation offers; it's also a great time to start introducing new ones. You might consider beginning a new Disciple Bible Study class during the week following this service. You could also introduce a variety of Bible-reading plans, many of which are available online and as applications for iPads, smart phones, and other mobile devices. (See the Bible Reading Chart in Appendix C, under 6. Tools and Helps, as well as on the CD-ROM in the back of this book.)

Close the message by inviting the congregation to pull out this week's commitment card and commit to deepening their relationship with God through an intentional Bible study plan, following the script provided in Part 2: Pastor.

Third Sunday:
"It's a Privilege to Be Here!"
Luke 19:45-48

This week we are challenging the people in your congregation to deepen their commitment to worship. Be careful that you don't simply "preach to the choir" and encourage people to come to church more often or fuss at people over low attendance. After all, most of the people listening are regular attenders! Instead, this is an opportunity to reflect on why worship is important and to invite people to be active participants in the worship experience, not simply passive spectators of a program.

The Gospel passage for today shows Jesus entering the Temple and driving out the money changers, then teaching in the Temple courts. In Luke's narrative (as well as Matthew's and Mark's, but not John's), this sequence of events occurred right after Jesus' triumphal entry on Palm Sunday and was one of the main reasons why the religious officials were upset with Jesus. This passage shows a rare instance of Jesus in a state of anger, so it presents an opportunity to talk about how passion is crucial to worship.

Many people in your congregation may be regular worship attenders, but they may never have thought about exactly why worshiping together is important. Worship could be a habit that began in childhood, or something they do "because you're supposed to." So, why is it important for Christians to gather together and worship on a regular basis? What difference does this group activity make in our lives?

One reason we worship as a group is that God did not create us only to be autonomous individuals; God created us to be in relationship with one another, and it's important to gather as a community to focus our minds and hearts on God. As crucial as individual devotional practices are, they are no substitute for worshiping as a community. Just as worship is enhanced by our individual devotional practices, those practices are enhanced by our corporate worship.

The corporate nature of faith is especially important because we live in a time when much of the technology meant to connect us often serves to make us feel more isolated. Ideally, corporate worship helps us to see and truly believe that we are not alone on the journey of life.

We also gather in worship to lift up and celebrate all that God is doing in the lives of the congregation, and to lift up those individuals who are struggling. That's why we take time in worship to pray specifically for the joys and concerns of our congregation.

Finally, we gather in worship to remind ourselves that God truly is the Lord of us all. Just as we need one another, we need God's active presence in our lives, and regularly gathering and proclaiming God's lordship as a community has a profound effect on our faith.

As in previous weeks, this may be a good time to lift up the lay testimony given this week about the life-changing effects of a commitment to regularly engage in worship. These stories or testimonies will serve to build a bridge between the high theological ideals we proclaim and the on-the-ground experiences of the people whom we are inviting to deepen their commitment. It is also a good opportunity to highlight the different worship experiences your congregation offers, if you have more than one, and the potential benefits of each experience.

Close the message by inviting the congregation to pull out this week's commitment card and commit to regular, intentional participation in corporate worship, following the script provided in Part 2: Pastor.

Fourth Sunday:
"You Shall Be My Witnesses"
Colossians 4:5-6

This week we are challenging the congregation to deepen their commitment to witness about their faith and invite others to begin the journey of Christian discipleship. You may want to refer back to the initial message in this series, when we challenged the congregation to make or deepen their commitment to Christ. It's important that the congregation understand that evangelism is not simply the job of church professionals or a select group of people. Witnessing and inviting are the job of every Christian.

Let's be honest: for some people, evangelism has a bad reputation. Lots of us have stories of uncomfortable or even painful encounters, when a super-aggressive person demanded to know if we had "prayed our prayer" and been saved, or stated that if we didn't agree with their understanding of the Gospel, we would burn in hell forever. You'll probably need to help your congregation understand that, while you are challenging them to take evangelism seriously, you are not asking them to be aggressive or obnoxious.

In this week's passage, Paul encourages the Colossians to be "wise in the way you act toward outsiders." Paul has been spending a lot of time in this letter encouraging Christians to live faithfully to what they know to be true and not to compromise their values, even when others around them may live in very different ways. Paul says nothing, however, about twisting people's arms and making them adopt our worldview. Nor does he say anything about being aggressive and unrelenting in telling others that their beliefs are wrong. Quite the opposite—Paul says to "make the most of every opportunity" and "let your every conversation be filled with grace." Paul is talking about evangelism through love, not through condemnation or even persuasion.

This is the right place to begin addressing how best to engage others in the community on issues of faith. Where do people in your community congregate? What are the most popular activities your neighbors engage in? It may be worth noting other evangelism efforts in your community that may have backfired and created negative feelings. Be sure not to criticize other churches specifically, but rather encourage your congregation to learn from the mistakes of others. The point of all of this is to think about how we can be the most loving, gracious witnesses to Christ in our communities.

Close your message by inviting the congregation to pull out this week's commitment card and prayerfully consider a commitment to witnessing, sharing faith, and inviting others to worship, following the script provided in Part 2: Pastor.

Fifth Sunday:
"Give Till It Feels Good"
Luke 21:1-4

This week we are challenging the congregation to make a deeper commitment to financial giving. If they are currently giving $5 a Sunday, we encourage them to step up to $10 or $20. If they are currently giving 2%, we ask them to step up to 3% or 4% this year, then continue to step up each year over the next three to six years until they have reached the Biblical minimum standard of the 10% tithe—not because the church needs money, but because as Christians our use of money should reflect our faith priorities.

Though some in the congregation may suspect that this week's theme is the real reason we've been talking about discipleship, it is important to emphasize that financial giving is simply a part—a very important part—of being a disciple of Jesus. If we are truly giving our whole lives over to Christ, then our resources and how we choose to use them has to be a big part of the conversation.

The Gospel passage from Luke shows Jesus and his disciples in the Temple courts, by the treasury where people make their offerings. Jesus is standing by the offering box, watching the amount each person puts in. A poor widow puts in a meager gift, in contrast to people who are putting in large sums of money and presumably are making a show of their generosity.

Notice that in Jesus' math, the widow gave more than the others. She gave all that she had, whereas the wealthy gave only a small portion of their excess money. You might say that Jesus apparently notices the balance in our checkbook as well as the size of our check. The 10% tithe is the great equalizer. If a poor person puts $35 into the offering and a wealthy person puts in $3,500, and both represent a 10% tithe of that week's income, then their gifts are equal according to Jesus' math. The call is for equal sacrifice, not equal gifts.

The widow in this story has much to teach all of us about love, trust, and the nature of God. She did not have much, but she gave all she had because she loved others beyond herself. She gave because she believed those coins could be multiplied by God for God's work better than by her. She knew that God could be trusted to be faithful beyond any bank or possession.

What do our gifts say about our ability to love? What does our checkbook say about our willingness to trust? Do we trust God at his word more than we are afraid of a bad economy? Are we controlled more by God's word or by the Wall Street Journal?

In trying to answer these questions honestly, we must take a long, hard look at our finances and consider whether there are changes we need to make. We must get our priorities in order. Such self-examination is rarely fun, but it benefits us greatly in the long run.

The decision made today by many of us will answer these questions. Could you give your last two coins? Could you begin to step up from 2% to 4% this year? Could you give a 10% tithe? Remember, for God so loved you . . . he gave.

Suggestions: Refer to this program's *Adult Readings and Study Book* and the preview book, *Six Steps to a Generous Life,* for examples of stories that may inspire your parishioners to tithe and for stories of households that stepped up to tithing over a three- to six-year period. Better yet, look within your own church for an example of a "modern-day widow" giving out of great love for God. It may be a child who gave all of her allowance, or a teacher who gave sacrificially on a teacher's salary. Nothing beats a genuine testimony or real-life story for demonstrating how giving can change a person's life.

Resist the temptation to mouth the kind of tired plea for financial help that many churches fall back on: "Your church needs money to accomplish the ministries described in our budget. Please give generously so that these ministries can be accomplished." Definitely resist the temptation to say: "Remember that our budget is going up 2% this year." Rather, the question in your sermon should be: "What percentage of your income do you feel God is calling you to give?" The issue here is not whether your church needs more money or not; the issue is that faithful disciples need and want to give a portion of their money for the work of the Lord.

Close the message by inviting the congregation to pull out this week's commitment card. Read it with them, fill it out together, and place all the cards in the commitment box.

Sixth Sunday
"Are You Ready to Get Blisters for Jesus?"
1 Corinthians 12:12-20

This week we are challenging the congregation to make a deeper commitment to spending time in active service to others. If you highlighted the ministries your church engages in last week, as part of the challenge to generous giving, you might start out this week by referencing that message and saying you'll be exploring these ministries further today. If your church decided to declare today Ministry Celebration Sunday, then you'll want to remind the congregation about the celebration activities that will be taking place after church.

Today's passage from First Corinthians says that different people have different gifts, and God intended it to be that way. Like parts of the body, each person has God-given abilities that contribute to a whole that is much greater than the sum of its parts. And, like a human body, when one part suffers, the rest of the church body suffers with it and must devote its energies to making the body whole again.

Some aspects of discipleship that we have discussed over the past few weeks, such as prayer, Bible reading, and worship, are, primarily inwardly focused. John Wesley, Anglican priest and founder of the eighteenth-century Methodist movement, called these "acts of piety." Wesley believed that acts of piety are crucial to Christian life but are nothing without "acts of mercy"—doing good in the world. Spending time in service to others blesses us, of course, often in much deeper ways than we realize; but it also reminds us that there is a world outside our own devotional lives that needs to be blessed by our efforts. Like intentionally giving, intentionally making time for service forces us to examine how we spend our resources (time, in this case) and to consider if we need to change in order to free up time for service.

When you take this opportunity to share information about the ministries of your church, make sure the ministries you pick engage a variety of different abilities, so that everybody in the congregation can find a way to participate. Some people may have the physical abilities to build houses for Habitat for Humanity. Others may have the ability to write notes or cards to visitors or sick church members. Still others may have artistic gifts that could be utilized in worship or other aspects of church life. If there are areas of giftedness that your church doesn't currently engage, this could be a great opportunity to begin new ministries.

As in past weeks, this can be a good opportunity to lift up the week's lay testimony about how serving in various ministry areas has changed people's lives. And, as in previous weeks, great care must be taken to make sure that God is the one being glorified, not individuals or groups.

Close the message by inviting the congregation to pull out this week's commitment card and prayerfully consider a commitment of time spent in service to others, following the script provided in Part 2: Pastor.

Appendix B.
More Program Ideas

Ways to Expand Committed to Christ

What about year two?

Repeat the entire process.

In Year one, the congregation understands that you are asking them to begin a journey "up the staircase," so they won't be surprised if the church continues the journey in subsequent years. In fact, they may be surprised if you don't use the program for four or five consecutive years, as you invite them to continue their journey toward faithful discipleship.

More Commitments?

In the second or third year, you may want to add to the seven commitments, perhaps asking for eight or nine commitments. Additional commitments could include Forgiveness, Missions, Family Relationships, Community Service, and Compassion.

Twelve-week Option

You could place additional emphasis on each of the original commitments if you expanded the program to twelve weeks instead of six. In this model, you would have an introductory Sunday or two, and then spend two weeks, rather than one, on each commitment.

If you choose this option, the commitment card, testimonies, and sermon would stay in place for both weeks, but the survey report and invitation would be only on the first week. The pastor would call for card signing and collection on the second Sunday.

This two-week pattern would be repeated for each of the six cards, for a total of twelve weeks instead of six.

Seven-month Option

We have had several congregations take an entire month for each commitment. August: accepting Jesus Christ as Lord and Savior; September: prayer; October: financial gifts (to coincide with most church's stewardship campaigns; November: service; December: Witness (like the shepherds and Wise Men, telling the good news of Jesus' birth); January: worship attendance (as a New Year's resolution); and February: Bible reading.

This option may be especially helpful in churches where a great number of the congregation are new disciples just beginning their faith journey. This extended emphasis functions in part as a discipleship system and helps new believers to better understand the expectations of faithful discipleship.

Twelve-month Option

After using Committed to Christ for two or three years, you might consider expanding the program and asking for twelve commitments. One model would be to emphasize a different commitment on the first Sunday of each month, perhaps receiving that month's commitment card when the congregation receives the Lord's Supper.

If your congregation comes to the front to kneel at a communion rail, that month's card could be left on the kneeling rail while they are there. In larger churches with multiple stations where bread and wine are brought forward, a third person carrying the Covenant Box could come along behind them.

Does it have to be an October campaign?

No, your stewardship campaign does not have to be in October.

While October and November have historically been the time for annual campaigns, you may find that the campaign can also be successful mid-January to mid-February. You could conduct Committed to Christ during Lent, being sure to complete the entire process before Easter Sunday.

Another window of opportunity is late April to late May, after taxes are filed and before the summer break.

New Small Groups?

Some of the seven commitments work well as topics for new short-term small groups, such as "Introducing Faith in Jesus Christ," "How to Pray," or Dave Ramsey's "Financial Peace." On those particular Sundays, the new group might be announced and opportunities given to enroll.

Optional Celebration Luncheon

Some congregations have held a Celebration Luncheon on the sixth Sunday. Since this luncheon will be held very close to Thanksgiving season, many congregations emphasize the Thanksgiving theme in the luncheon menu and decorations.

If the Celebration Luncheon is held, the Celebration Team secures reservations for the luncheon at the same time that they make telephone calls about Ministry Celebration Sunday.

If you decide to have the Celebration Luncheon, the Steward needs to decide on its format and enlist the Celebration Team's support. You may need to adjust the advance letter that goes to potential Celebration Team members, as well as the content of the training meeting with the Celebration Team members to include the Celebration Luncheon responsibilities.

In the initial meeting of the Celebration Team, you may want to form a separate Celebration Luncheon task group.

To encourage attendance and remove any excuse for not coming, the Celebration Luncheon should not be a typical churchwide potluck. Chose from some of the following:

- Thanksgiving meal, with all the food prepared by the Celebration Team.
- A fully catered Thanksgiving meal, paid for by an individual or by the Celebration Team. Do not charge members to attend the luncheon.
- One church asked each Celebration Team member, following a Thanksgiving theme, to prepare any food they wished for two tables. Team members set the food on the tables, family style, immediately prior to the luncheon, then served as "wait staff" for their two tables. As the congregation entered the fellowship hall, they had the privilege of choosing the table they preferred. The following year, the Steward chose the menu, and each team member prepared those menu items at home and brought them to the church, again serving two tables each, so that the food was almost identical at every table in the room.

Divide up tasks among the Celebration Team such as setup, table decorations, cooking, serving, and cleanup. Resist the temptation to hire a catering service. The primary goal here is to involve your people actively in the program, giving them buy-in and the opportunity to serve.

At the worship service on the fifth Sunday of the program, in addition to announcing Ministry Celebration Sunday, the Steward or pastor would invite the congregation to the Celebration Luncheon, using words such as:

Good Morning! In your chair this morning you found a Celebration Luncheon reservation card. We are hoping that every family in the church will be present next Sunday, November ____, for the luncheon. We have a team of folks who are doing all the cooking, so you don't need to bring anything. The Celebration Team is so eager for all of you to be present that we will telephone everyone we don't hear from this morning. So do fill out the reservation card and place it in the offering plate.

If you follow this luncheon pattern, the Celebration Team would only call the households that have not made a luncheon reservation.

Small-attendance Churches

As you read about the program, you may be thinking, "My church has only twenty people. This is just too much!"

Don't panic. Committed to Christ can be adjusted for any size church.

Perhaps in your small-attendance church you would use only a couple of program features: (1) ask your pastor to preach a six-sermon series during October and November; and (2) each of those six Sundays, use the commitment card that matches the sermon.

You can decide which portions of the program fit the unique personality of your small-attendance church.

Do Members Have to Sign a Card?

It is amazing how many congregations are hesitant to sign a commitment card, and refuse to allow the Finance Committee or pastor to institute the use of a commitment card. Today, with such widespread use of debit and credit cards, church members are asked to sign their name countless times.

We do not recommend removing the signature line on the commitment cards.

However, if your congregation is about to reject the use of Committed to Christ simply because of the signature line on each of the six cards, there is a simple answer: when introducing the card each Sunday (and in the congregation letter) make signing the card an option not a requirement, or customize the six cards and simply leave the signature line off the card.

Appendix C.
Using the CD-ROM

The CD-ROM inside the back cover of this *Program Guide* contains a variety of useful documents, samples, and tools. These are described on the following pages, along with instructions regarding how to use them.

You are welcome to print out and use any of the CD-ROM documents for your church program. Some churches may have the expertise and software to handle the documents themselves; others may prefer to enlist the help of a local printer or graphic designer.

However you choose to use the documents, we trust they will help present the program more effectively and take your congregation to the next level of commitment to Christ.

CD-ROM Contents

All items listed below are on the CD-ROM.
*Items are printed in this appendix.

1. *Program Guide* Sections
- Introduction
- 1. Program Approach and Structure
- 2. Commitment to Christ
- 3. The Six Steps
- 4. Worship and Sermons
- 5. Small Groups
- 6. Prayers and Devotions
- 7. Why Committed to Christ?
- 14. Sample Schedule

2. Brochure, Banner, and Graphics
- Six-step Brochure
- Banner
- Poster
- Flyer
- Logos

3. Commitment Cards
- Introductory Week. Commitment to Jesus Christ
- Week 1. Prayer
- Week 2. Bible Reading
- Week 3. Worship

- Week 4. Witness
- Week 5. Financial Giving
- Week 6. Service
- Youth
- Children

4. Letters
- *Churchwide Introductory Letter
- *Churchwide Immediate Follow-up Letter
- *Churchwide 30-day Follow-up Letter
- *Invitation Letter to Pastor's Coffee
- *Invitation Letter to Potential Celebration Team Members
- *Monthly Thank You Letter
- *Cover Letter - Devotions

5. Phone Contacts
- *Ministry Celebration Sunday - Phone Script
- *Ministry Celebration Sunday - Instructions and Call List

6. Tools and Helps
- Service Opportunities – Bulletin Insert
- Including New and Potential Members
- Luncheon Reservation Card
- You've Been Asked to Share a Personal Testimony
- Bible Reading Chart
- Music Suggestions
- Follow-up Resources

7. Survey
- Survey – Short Version
- Survey – Long Version
- Survey – Extended Version
- Survey – Tally Sheet
- Survey – Weekly Report
- Survey – New Members Class

8. Task Lists
- Pastor
- Steward
- Coordinator
- Celebration Team

9. PowerPoint and Videos

1.

Program Guide Sections

Sections of this *Program Guide* will serve as useful articles and handouts for those involved in the program. With that in mind, the following *Program Guide* sections appear in PDF format for you to distribute. These black-and-white pages can be printed out onto 8½ x 11" sheets in your church office.

- Introduction
- 1. Program Approach and Structure
- 2. Commitment to Christ
- 3. The Six Steps
- 4. Worship and Sermons
- 5. Small Groups
- 6. Prayers and Devotions
- 7. Why Committed to Christ?
- 14. Sample Schedule

2.

BROCHURE, BANNER, AND GRAPHICS

The Six-step Brochure is an important tool in presenting the program to your congregation. It provides a helpful overview of commitment to Christ and the six steps, describing the commitment levels in each step and what they build toward, along with inspirational Scriptures. Print out the brochure on both sides of an 8½ x 14" sheet and fold it into quarters, with the cover panel facing out.

In addition to the brochure, a number of items for promoting and publicizing your program are provided here, including a banner, a poster, a flyer, and a variety of logos and graphic elements, with which you and your printer can create items tailored to the needs of your particular congregation.

- Six-step Brochure
- Banner
- Poster
- Flyer
- Logos

3.

COMMITMENT CARDS

Your congregation will be studying and filling out commitment cards during every week of the program. The cards ask questions and provide a wide range of answer options, ranging from no commitment to deep and lifelong commitment. Members of your congregation will use these cards to take stock of where they are in each facet of Christian life, then commit to moving one step higher.

The commitment cards are presented three-to-a-page. Cut them apart after printing. When reproducing the commitment cards, you might consider using a sturdy card stock that displays color well.

- Introductory Week. Commitment to Jesus Christ
- Week 1. Prayer
- Week 2. Bible Reading
- Week 3. Worship
- Week 4. Witness
- Week 5. Financial Giving
- Week 6. Service
- Youth
- Children

4.
LETTERS

Communication with your church members and teams is essential for the program to succeed, and letters play an important part in that communication. For each letter listed below, you'll find one page of description and instructions, followed by the letter itself.

The letters are presented in Word format on the CD-ROM. Feel free to edit and adjust them for your particular congregation. You will also find the letters printed on the following pages, in case you would like to photocopy them.

- Churchwide Introductory Letter
- Churchwide Immediate Follow-up Letter
- Churchwide 30-day Follow-up Letter
- Invitation Letter to Pastor's Coffee
- Invitation Letter to Potential Celebration Team Members
- Monthly Thank You Letter
- Cover Letter - Devotions

Committed to Christ
Churchwide Introductory Letter

What

Introduces the program to the congregation

When

After the Celebration Team has been finalized and their first training session completed, and a few weeks before the program begins

Who

Coordinator and church staff

How

Change text of letter as needed

- if you decide to hold a churchwide luncheon on Ministry Celebration Sunday

In addition to the letter, you'll want to include:

- Six-step Brochure
- Set of Commitment Cards

For churches that want to delve deeper, consider including one of the following:

- *Adult Readings and Study Book*
- Preview Book: *Six Steps to a Generous Life*
- Devotional Book: *40 Devotions for a Generous Life*

Dear Friends of _____ Church,

What does it mean to be a disciple of Jesus Christ?
What does the Lord expect of me?
What "holy habits" should I cultivate in my life?

For six Sundays beginning in October, our entire church family is invited to enter a season of decision and commitment toward the goal of becoming fully devoted disciples of Jesus Christ. The theme will be *Committed to Christ: Six Steps to a Generous Life.*

We are hoping that every household will be present every Sunday during this season so that we can each commit to climb one step closer toward this goal. We will dedicate ourselves to the Lord and obey what the Lord has commanded, in a spirit of gratitude for all that we have received.

On an introductory Sunday at the start of the program, we will be asked to make or renew our personal commitment to Christ. Each of the six Sundays following will emphasize a different area of faithful Christian discipleship: prayer, Bible reading, worship, witness, financial giving, and service.

We have enclosed a Six-step Brochure that will describe the program and show the various levels of commitment, ranging from limited commitment to full and unlimited commitment. We have also enclosed a set of commitment cards that you will be invited to complete and turn in during worship on each Sunday of the program. This means that no one will stop by your home.

To celebrate what God is doing here at _____ Church, the program will culminate in a special Ministry Celebration Sunday, when all the ministries of the church will be lifted up through music, banners, and procession.

May God bless each of us as we commit together to become a fully devoted disciple of Jesus Christ.

Grace,

[Name]
Steward of Committed to Christ Program

Committed to Christ
Churchwide Immediate Follow-up Letter

What

Reports the results of the program to the congregation

When

Immediately after Ministry Celebration Sunday, the final Sunday of the program

Who

The Mailing Task Group

How

In addition to the letter, you'll want to include:

- Six-step Brochure
- Set of Commitment Cards
- Stamped, self-addressed return envelope

Dear Friends of _____ Church,

We wanted you to know that Committed to Christ, our fall discipleship emphasis, was a big success. We had a great response in the number of commitment cards turned in during the six weeks of the program.

_____ commitment cards were signed in worship with the following decisions:

_____ commitments to grow closer in faith to Jesus Christ
_____ commitments to grow in daily prayer
_____ commitments to grow in daily Bible reading
_____ commitments to grow closer to perfect worship attendance
_____ commitments to grow in witnessing to others
_____ commitments to grow in financial giving to the Lord's church
_____ commitments to grow toward serving the Lord willingly with our hands

If you have turned in all your commitment cards, thank you!

If you have not yet turned in all the cards, it is not too late to join with the rest of the church family in making these commitments. We've enclosed a set of cards and a self-addressed return envelope for your convenience. When we receive your cards, they will be placed in the locked covenant box on the altar.

Your generosity in prayers, Bible reading, attendance, witness, financial gifts, and service will help our church to continue the wonderful ministries here, and to give our fair share of support to our ministries around the world.

Thank you for making commitments to climb one step in your discipleship this year.

Grace,

[Name]
Steward of Committed to Christ Program

P.S. An entire household may use the same commitment card by placing initials next to the commitments you wish to make.

Committed to Christ
Churchwide 30-day Follow-up Letter

What

Reports the results of the program to the congregation (the same group that received the Churchwide Immediate Follow-up Letter)

When

Thirty days after Ministry Celebration Sunday, the final Sunday of the program

Who

The Mailing Task Group

How

In addition to the letter, you'll want to include:

- Six-step Brochure
- Set of Commitment Cards
- No response envelope is needed, since households have received multiple opportunities to respond

After this letter is mailed, the Financial Secretary may want to send a letter to those who made financial commitments, to confirm the amount of their pledge.

Dear Friends of _____ Church,

　　We had a great response in the number of commitment cards turned in during our fall discipleship emphasis, Committed to Christ: Six Steps to a Generous Life.

　　Almost _____ commitment cards were signed in worship with the following decisions:

　　　　_____ commitments to grow closer in faith to Jesus Christ
　　　　_____ commitments to grow in daily prayer
　　　　_____ commitments to grow in daily Bible reading
　　　　_____ commitments to grow closer to perfect worship attendance
　　　　_____ commitments to grow in witnessing to others
　　　　_____ commitments to grow in financial giving to the Lord's church
　　　　_____ commitments to grow toward serving the Lord willingly with our hands

　　Your generosity in prayers, Bible reading, attendance, witness, financial gifts, and service will help our church to continue the wonderful ministries here, and to give our fair share of support to our ministries around the world.

　　Thank you for making commitments to climb one step in your discipleship this year.

　　　　　　　　　　　　　　　　Grace,

　　　　　　　　　　　　　　　　[Name]
　　　　　　　　　　　　　　　　Steward of Committed to Christ Program

P.S. If you made a financial commitment during Committed to Christ, the Financial Secretary will be sending you a letter to confirm your pledge.

Committed to Christ
Invitation Letter to Pastor's Coffee

What

This is a wonderful idea from Bill Easum's little book, *The Missing Piece*. The idea is to divide the entire church into small groups and invite them to the pastor's home for dessert and coffee. My personal experience is that over 80% of those who attended these events not only completed the commitment cards but also increased their financial commitment to the church's general fund.

Where

The location makes a difference. It communicates the pastor's personal support for the program. For cases in which the pastor's home is not available, the small groups can convene in the church parlor. In most cases the pastor's home will not be equipped to handle the childcare. While the coffee is at the pastor's home, the childcare will be provided at the church.

When

Keep these meetings short (under an hour). As guests arrive, serve dessert and coffee. A few minutes later the pastor welcomes the group, then shares a personal vision for the future of the church (ten minutes or less). Next, the Steward or Stewards briefly give an overview of the program and distribute all the commitment cards (three minutes each). The Lay Leader or Council chair asks those present to "climb up one step" in each area, emphasizing that increased financial support will help make this vision become a reality. The pastor closes the time with a prayer and invites the guests to take a second serving of dessert and visit for a while.

Who

In congregations with worship attendance under three hundred, it might be possible to invite every household to attend one of several coffees. In larger churches, the invitation list might be limited. You might decide to invite the Committed to Christ team to attend, and ask each of the team members to bring two congregational leaders (church officers, small group leaders, Sunday school class leaders, or leaders from each ministry area). In this way you'll expand the number of leaders who receive the invitation from the pastor to make advance commitments to step up.

How

The invitation is more effective if mailed in a "wedding invitation" size envelope (A6) with the invitation printed on appropriately sized card stock. The front of the card can read "An Invitation."

Dear Friends of _____ Church,

        _____ and I are deeply grateful that God has led you to become a member of the our church family. You are an important part of this church. We have prayed together for our church; we have worked together; and God is blessing our church abundantly.

        We believe that the success of Committed to Christ: Six Steps to a Generous Life is vital for our continued growth and ministry. Each of us in the church will play an important role in the success of this program.

        With this in mind, _____ and I are inviting you to our home on the evening of _____ for coffee and dessert, to share our vision for the church and our hopes for the Committed to Christ program. We know that you are busy, but we ask that you to make this a high priority. Please RSVP within the next couple of days by calling the church office at _____. Also, let us know if you need childcare. If you call after hours, you can leave a message.

        Surely our church has one of the greatest opportunities for ministry of any church in town. *You* are vital to that growing ministry! We have a great church because people like you are committed to reaching people for Christ. We are counting on your continued help and support.

        We look forward to seeing you at our home and hearing your hopes and dreams for our church in a more personal setting.

                              Grace,

                              [Name]
                              Pastor of _____ Church

Date:
Time:
Place:
Childcare: (Provided at the church)

Committed to Christ
Invitation Letter to Potential Celebration Team Members

What

Sent to the people the Steward and pastor have agreed will be invited to join the Celebration Team

When

August, or about two months before the program begins

Who

Office staff, directed by the pastor and Steward

How

Change text of the letter as needed:

- if you prefer a reply postcard or e-mail to a phone call response
- if you decide to hold a churchwide luncheon on Ministry Celebration Sunday

Dear _____,

We need your help.

We are looking for _____ people to serve as Celebration Team members for the fall discipleship emphasis, Committed to Christ: Six Steps to a Generous Life. We invite you to be part of our team.

The job is simple but very important.

First, we invite you to be a leader in our church and to take seriously the invitation to grow one step closer to

- accept Jesus Christ as Lord and Savior
- pray daily
- read the Bible daily
- attend worship faithfully
- witness your faith to others
- give significantly and proportionately
- serve willingly

If you accept that invitation, we ask you to attend two training sessions:

1. First training session: Choose either Sunday, _____, at _____ o'clock; or Monday, _____, at _____ o'clock. At this one-hour gathering, you will receive the details and have an opportunity to ask questions.

2. Second training session: Choose either Sunday, _____, at _____ o'clock; or Monday, _____, at _____ o'clock. At this one-hour session, you will learn how to contact members of the congregation, asking them to be present in worship on Ministry Celebration Sunday. You will be asked to make ten to twelve phone calls.

Please call the church office and let us know if you will be accepting our invitation to be part of the Celebration Team and, if so, what training sessions you would like to attend. If we don't hear from you in a few days, one of us will be calling to follow up.

Grace,

[Name]
Steward of Committed to Christ Program

Committed to Christ
Monthly Thank You Letter

What

A thank you letter should be sent to each household on a regular basis. This thank you letter is attached to the individual giving record.

When

Monthly, or every other month

Who

The Mailing Task Group

Why

Without a thank you letter, the giving statement looks like a bill or past-due notice. This thank you letter allows each ministry area, if it so chooses, to give a year-to-date summary of lives changed in Jesus' name.

How

- Be sure to include a copy of the individual giving record.
- See the sample below. Please use and adapt the letter as needed, filling in the correct information for your particular church.
- Consider including the Committed to Christ logo (see Brochure, Banner, and Graphics) and photos from the ministries of your church.

Thank you!

**Your generosity has helped to provide many important ministries
in the name of our Lord Jesus Christ.**

So far this year…

- We have held _____ worship services, including Monday evening worship and the Sunday morning praise service
- The Lord's Supper has been served _____ times to _____ worshipers
- We witnessed _____ baptisms, and _____ persons reaffirmed their faith in Jesus Christ
- We welcomed _____ new households into our church family
- Youth ministry continued to grow and bless our 5th through 12th graders
- Children's ministry for ages 2-11 expanded to include Wednesday and Sunday evenings
- We enjoyed the addition of an adult drama team and a praise band
- Our handbell groups have expanded our music ministry
- The new children's choir, the adult choir, and our Grace Singers continue to practice diligently
- Marriages were strengthened, and the grieving were comforted
- Forgiveness and hope were received, and salvation from God was discovered
- Our faith was strengthened through the Commited to Christ program
- Literature for _____ Sunday school class sessions was purchased
- _____ of our youth went on a mission trip this summer
- _____ adults went on a mission trip to Haiti this fall
- _____ invitations were mailed to local residents
- _____ weekly newsletters were mailed
- _____ missionaries were supported around the world

Committed to Christ
Cover Letter – Devotions

What

A cover letter introducing the devotional book, *Committed to Christ: 40 Devotions for a Generous Life*, to the congregation

When

Sent with the devotional book when churches purchase a copy of the book for each household in the congregation

Why

To encourage families to use the devotional book during the weeks of the program as part of their family devotional time

Who

Coordinator and church staff can send the books and cover letters

Dear Friends of _____ Church,

Greetings! We are excited to join you on your spiritual journey during the Committed to Christ program, as you read *Committed to Christ: 40 Devotions for a Generous Life*. This small devotional book was written to facilitate growth in the Christian life, and can be used within family settings. Please consider the following ways to make use of this devotional book in your home:

- Begin or end each day with a reading from the devotional book. Find a comfortable place and commit to making this a habit during the program. Apply what you read as you seek to be a better spouse or parent.
- Use this devotional book as a way of teaching your children the value of daily Bible reading, prayer, and reflection. Parents, show your children the book and tell them how you will use it each day.
- If your children are able, read together as a family. Each devotional entry consists of three parts: a Scripture reading, a meditation, and a closing prayer. If there are three or more members in your household, assign different portions to different individuals and read aloud.
- At the close of each section, you'll find an invitation to make a commitment (Taking a Step). Plan a family conversation, perhaps during a meal, during which you can discuss how each person will commit to prayer, worship attendance, witness, and so on. In this way, the devotional book can be used to help establish the practice of spiritual conversations within the home.
- Create time for questions and further exploration of the Bible readings. Keep a Bible nearby while you read or discuss. If something you read captures your imagination or sparks a question, explore it with your spouse or family. Spiritual growth happens best in community.

May you be richly blessed as you seek to draw nearer to God in the weeks to come.

Grace,

[Name]
Steward of Committed to Christ Program

5.
PHONE CONTACTS

In addition to sending letters, your team will make many phone calls, contacting every church member and prospective member in order to encourage attendance and participation in the program. One of the most important events that will require prior phone contact is the Ministry Celebration Sunday, on the final week of the program.

Documents in this section include a phone script for team members to use when calling about Ministry Celebration Sunday, along with instructions for organizing the calls and a place for team members to list the people they will be calling.

Like the letters, these documents are presented in Word format on the CD-ROM. Feel free to edit and adjust them for your particular congregation. The letters can also be found printed on the following pages, for photocopying.

- Ministry Celebration Sunday - Phone Script
- Ministry Celebration Sunday - Instructions and Call List

Committed to Christ
Ministry Celebration Sunday
Phone Script

Note: If you decide to hold a Thanksgiving theme luncheon on Ministry Celebration Sunday, these telephone calls are not only to encourage attendance but to obtain reservations for the luncheon.

- In order to plan phone calls for Ministry Celebration Sunday, the Celebration Team should meet at least a week ahead of time, preferably on the evening of the fifth Sunday. The meeting's purpose is to tell the team about the telephone invitations they will be making to invite every household to come to church on Ministry Celebration Sunday.
- At that meeting, the Steward or pastor will give a brief (two- or three-minute) inspirational address. Then the Steward will review the task: to telephone every household in the church family, inviting them to be present the following Sunday for Celebrating Ministry Sunday.
- The Steward will ask that these contacts be made Sunday, Monday, Tuesday, and Wednesday, and that team members email or telephone the results back to the Steward before 7:00 p.m. on Thursday. (Keep a of record of the names each team member chooses to call. This will enable you to reassign the task if they fail to make their calls.)
- How do you divide up the names to call? We've found it works well to place church mailing labels (including phone numbers) on 3x5 cards. Spread out the cards on tables, the altar, or kneeling rail and invite team members to choose the cards of people they would like to call. Encourage them to pick five cards of people they know and five others. After this selection process, distribute any remaining cards. Then each team member should write the names they chose on the report form and leave it with you.
- The script for the calls is simple. You can demonstrate it at the meeting:

> Hello, _____, this is _____ from _____ Church.
> This week we are making telephone calls to every household related to the church, reminding everyone that this coming Sunday is Ministry Celebration Sunday. We are hoping every household will be present.
> We will have great music and will celebrate all the ministries of the church.
> I am looking forward to seeing you this Sunday.

- If team members encounter an answering machine, instruct them to leave that same message. In some cases, leaving a voice mail can be more effective than a personal conversation. Encourage team members to avoid making phone calls past 7:30 p.m. in the evening. (That cutoff time might be adjusted depending on your particular congregation.)

- If membership rolls haven't been updated in a while, you may hear something like, "I don't know why you are calling us. We attend a different church now." In that case, the caller can respond,

  > I didn't know that. Please excuse this call. Let me be sure I have the right information for our church office. You said that you are no longer members at our church but are members at _____ now. Can you tell me the approximate date so I can notify our office?
  >
  > [Then end with:] "I am so pleased that you are active in a church. Please excuse this call.

- When making this many phone calls, it will not be unusual to catch some people who are having a bad day or are angry at the church. If they start to express frustration or anger, don't argue or agree. Just wait for them to pause for a breath (and they will have to breath at some point!) and offer, "I hear what you are saying. Would you like me to have the pastor call you?" They will answer, "No." At that point, quickly end the conversation by saying, "We hope you can be present this Sunday for Ministry Celebration Sunday. Good evening."

Committed to Christ
Ministry Celebration Sunday
Instructions and Call List

- Our goal is to secure a promise from every church member to attend worship on Ministry Celebration Sunday.
- Your job as a Celebration Team member is to pray for the people on your list, and then invite them to attend worship.
- Please make telephone contact with every person on your list on Sunday, Monday, Tuesday, or Wednesday.
- Report back by 7:00 p.m. on Thursday evening, _____ .
  Steward's phone _____
  Steward's e-mail _____

- -

I have selected the cards for the following households:

1. _____
2. _____
3. _____
4. _____
5. _____
6. _____
7. _____
8. _____
9. _____
10. _____

Print your name here: _____

Committed to Christ
Ministry Celebration Sunday
Instructions and Call List

- Our goal is to secure a promise from every church member to attend worship on Ministry Celebration Sunday.
- Your job as a Celebration Team member is to pray for the people on your list, and then invite them to attend worship.
- Please make telephone contact with every person on your list on Sunday, Monday, Tuesday, or Wednesday.
- Report back by 7:00 p.m. on Thursday evening, _____ .
  Steward's phone _____
  Steward's e-mail _____

- -

I have selected the cards for the following households:

1. _____
2. _____
3. _____
4. _____
5. _____
6. _____
7. _____
8. _____
9. _____
10. _____

Print your name here: _____

6.

TOOLS AND HELPS

This section includes a variety of tools that can be useful during the program, ranging from a bulletin insert regarding service opportunities, to a Bible reading chart, to music suggestions and a list of follow-up resources.

- Service Opportunities – Bulletin Insert
- Including New and Potential Members
- Luncheon Reservation Card
- You've Been Asked to Share a Personal Testimony
- Bible Reading Chart
- Music Suggestions
- Follow-up Resources

7.

SURVEY

One of the most important parts of the program is an initial survey administered in the months leading up to the program, to establish some statistics and a baseline against which you can measure commitments made once the program begins. You'll also find the survey information helpful in planning church programs and ministries for the future.

To give you maximum flexibility, we are providing three versions of the survey: a short version (1 page), a long version (1½ pages), and an extended version (2 pages). Look over these versions and decide which one will work best for your congregation. Since you may want to tailor these surveys, a Word document for each version is provided here.

A tally sheet is provided as well, to help you total and review the responses, as well as information and a script for presenting results to the congregation each week and a suggestion for making use of the survey information in your new member classes.

- Survey – Short Version
- Survey – Long Version
- Survey – Extended Version
- Survey – Tally Sheet
- Survey – Weekly Report
- Survey – New Members Class

8.
Task Lists

When recruiting leaders for the program, it's important to describe responsibilities and schedules verbally; however, verbal communication is best followed up and reinforced by handing the recruits a list of the tasks they'll be asked to perform and a schedule showing when those tasks will take place. This way, recruits can take the information home, check it against their calendars, discuss it with family members, and give you a thoughtful, informed answer. Our hope is that the answer will be yes!

Tasks lists and schedules are provided for the following program leaders:

- Pastor
- Steward
- Coordinator
- Celebration Team

9.
POWERPOINT AND VIDEOS

Before you recruit, before you plan, before you begin the Committed to Christ program, you will need to convince key groups in your congregation that the program will benefit your church and its members. To help you with this important task, we have provided a Power-Point program describing the program and its benefits. Please feel free to edit and adapt the program for your own particular congregation.

We have also provided sermon lead-in videos and a program preview video, in MP4 and windows Media Video (WMV) formats.

- PowerPoint Program
- Video Files

ACKNOWLEDGMENTS

I am indebted to many people for inspiring this program and for the basic pattern of inviting individuals to journey toward faithful discipleship.

The program was born during a conversation with Dr. Norman Neaves, former pastor of the United Methodist Church of the Servant in Oklahoma City, Oklahoma. Norman was uncomfortable simply asking his congregation to make financial commitments and was seeking ways to invite them to make a more comprehensive commitment to follow Jesus Christ faithfully. I am also grateful for the numerous illustrations he shared with me that have helped to communicate a welcoming invitation within each of the six steps to a generous life.

Matt Kelley, Frank Ramirez, and Ben Simpson have done outstanding jobs in writing, respectively, the sermon starters, leader guide, and devotional book and CD-ROM that are included in the Committed to Christ program. I am grateful for their contributions and insights, which have expanded the usefulness and effectiveness of the program.

I am also indebted to the wonderful people and staff of Grace United Methodist Church in Conway, Arkansas, where the program was first designed and practiced. They gave hundreds of hours to field test the program. Their generosity and commitment are a great inspiration to me.

Clif Christopher, founder of Horizons Stewardship, has a wealth of experience with Christian financial stewardship in local churches and institutions from California to Washington, D.C. Clif and his staff helped to redesign the program so that it offered flexibility in various-size congregations and options for expanding the program in the second and following years. Staff member Scott McKenzie suggested the use of a banner processional for Ministry Celebration Sunday. Clif and his team of ministry strategists have conducted hundreds of successful capital funds campaigns across the United States, including three campaigns in churches when I was the senior pastor.

Herb Miller wrote an absolutely wonderful thirty-day program called *The New Consecration Sunday Stewardship Program.* If you have used Herb Miller's program before, you'll see that Committed to Christ is a natural follow-up for the next three or four years.

Bill Easum, in his booklet *The Missing Piece,* shares powerful insights about stewardship and includes the idea of the pastor hosting small groups of members in the parsonage for a personal invitation for members to grow as stewards.

I am grateful to Susan Salley, Ron Kidd, Marcia Myatt, Jennifer Rogers, Sally Sharpe, Tracey Craddock, Alan Vermilye, John Clark, and Sonia Worsham of Abingdon Press for their professionalism in preparing *Committed to Christ* for publication. They were abundantly helpful and offered invaluable assistance, support, and guidance.

I also extend my gratitude to the countless individuals—too many to list—who have supported this program through their commitment, enthusiasm, and dedicated hard work.

Most of all, I am grateful to my wife, Marcia, whose faith has strengthened my personal commitment to Christ and who has provided a faith-filled environment to raise our children—an environment so rich that today both our sons are living their commitment to Christ in their own households, teaching their young children to pray and live holy lives. What a blessing to see my wife sitting in church on Sunday, surrounded by our sons, their wives, and our four grandchildren.

NOTES

1. Bob Farr with Kay Kotan, Renovate or Die: 10 Ways to Focus Your Church on Mission. (Nashville: Abingdon Press, 2011), p. 1.

2. "Barna Examines Trends in 14 Religious Factors over 20 Years (1991–2011), Barna Group, February 10, 2011, http://www.barna.org/faith-spirituality/504-barna-examines-trends-in-14-religious-factors-over-20-years-1991-to-2011

3. John Wesley, "The Scripture Way of Salvation" (sermon 43, May 26, 1758). Text from the 1872 edition, Thomas Jackson, editor.

4. Disciple I DVD Set Revised: Becoming Disciples Through Bible Study. (Nashville: Abingdon Press, 2005), Albert Outler quoted in interview with Richard Wilkie.

5. The Church of England, "Worship," February 10, 2012, http://www.churchofengland.org/prayer-worship/worship.aspx

6. George A. Buttrick, The Parables of Jesus (New York: Harper & Row, 1928). The statistical counts are the opinions of Russell Blowers, "Minister's Memo," The Ninety-First Edition, Volume 36, No. 11 (November 1989), newsletter of the Ninety-First Street Christian Church, 6049 East Ninety-First Street, Indianapolis, Indiana 46250-1398. Quoted by Herb Miller in "Herb Miller's Nuggets: Volume 31," at http://www.godslove.org/resources/pdfs/herb_miller.pdf (February 10, 2010).

7. William M. Easum, "The Missing Piece: Stewardship for the 1990s." (Port Aransas TX: 21st Century Strategies, 1990).

8. The United Methodist Church, Call to Action: Steering Team Report (Nashville, 2010), Appendix 1: Towers Watson Report, p. 35.

9. The United Methodist Church, Call to Action: Steering Team Report (Nashville, 2010), Appendix 1: Towers Watson Report, p. 16.

10. Dean R. Hoge, Charles Zech, Patrick McNamara, and Michael J. Donahue, Money Matters: Personal Giving in American Churches. (Louisville: Westminster John Knox Press, 1996.) pp. 98-100, 183-203.

11. Herb Miller, New Consecration Sunday. (Nashville: Abingdon Press, 2007) pp. 5-6.

CD-ROM TABLE OF CONTENTS

1. *Program Guide* Sections
   - Introduction
   - 1. Program Approach and Structure
   - 2. Commitment to Christ
   - 3. The Six Steps
   - 4. Worship and Sermons
   - 5. Small Groups
   - 6. Prayers and Devotions
   - 7. Why Committed to Christ?
   - 14. Sample Schedule

2. Brochure, Banner, and Graphics
   - Six-step Brochure
   - Banner
   - Poster
   - Flyer
   - Logos

3. Commitment Cards
   - Introductory Week. Commitment to Jesus Christ
   - Week 1. Prayer
   - Week 2. Bible Reading
   - Week 3. Worship
   - Week 4. Witness
   - Week 5. Financial Giving
   - Week 6. Service
   - Youth
   - Children

4. Letters
   - *Churchwide Introductory Letter
   - *Churchwide Immediate Follow-up Letter
   - *Churchwide 30-day Follow-up Letter
   - *Invitation Letter to Pastor's Coffee
   - *Invitation Letter to Potential Celebration Team Members
   - *Monthly Thank You Letter
   - *Cover Letter - Devotions

5. Phone Contacts
   - *Ministry Celebration Sunday - Phone Script
   - *Ministry Celebration Sunday - Instructions and Call List

6. Tools and Helps
   - Service Opportunities – Bulletin Insert
   - Including New and Potential Members
   - Luncheon Reservation Card
   - You've Been Asked to Share a Personal Testimony
   - Bible Reading Chart
   - Music Suggestions
   - Follow-up Resources

7. Survey
   - Survey – Short Version
   - Survey – Long Version
   - Survey – Extended Version
   - Survey – Tally Sheet
   - Survey – Weekly Report
   - Survey – New Members Class

8. Task Lists
   - Pastor
   - Steward
   - Coordinator
   - Celebration Team

9. PowerPoint and Videos